OLD COPENHAGEN FIGURE GROUP.
Lady and gentleman in contemporary costume.
Frontispiece.

Chats on
Royal Copenhagen Porcelain

BY
ARTHUR HAYDEN

KNIGHT OF THE DANNEBROG

WITH FRONTISPIECE AND 56 FULL-PAGE ILLUSTRATIONS
TOGETHER WITH
ILLUSTRATED TABLES OF MARKS

TO

WILLIAM PETERSEN, Esq.

AS A TOKEN OF APPRECIATION OF HIS PATRIOTISM AND GENEROSITY IN
FURTHERING THE INTERESTS OF ART AND STIMULATING ANGLO-DANISH FRIENDSHIP.

PREFACE

"A good wine needs no bush" is an old English proverb, and this is essentially true in regard to the art of the Royal Copenhagen Porcelain Factory. The late M. Louis Solon, in preparing his colossal bibliographic work on *Ceramic Literature*, called my attention to the curious fact that a small pamphlet (some four and a half by five inches square, of fourteen pages) written by me originally for the *Artist* magazine in 1902, and reprinted as a guide to the Royal Copenhagen porcelain exhibit at the Wolverhampton Exhibition in 1902, was marked "rare" and being sold to collectors for five shillings. M. Solon, with his usual perspicacity, added: "It looks as though, in its course from East to West, ceramic painting has deserted its old home to take refuge in the North. *C'est du Nord aujourd'hui que nous vient la lumière!*"

In 1911, *Royal Copenhagen Porcelain: Its History and Development from the Eighteenth Century to the Present Day* was issued by my publisher, who in bringing out this sumptuous monograph fell under the spell of the beauty of Copenhagen art. That volume appealed to connoisseurs and collectors and was welcomed both here, on the Continent, and in America.

It has been thought desirable, in view of the limited circulation of that volume, to issue a popular edition, which is here presented in a slightly abridged form with none of the essentials omitted. Many of the illustrations have not found their way into this gallery. But a brave array of pictures is given to convey to the general reader, and to those who have not perused the larger volume, the chief characteristics of Royal Copenhagen porcelain, and indicate reasons why this factory is now regarded as the leading factory in Europe.

How many of the great factories of the world can claim two great epochs in their history? But Copenhagen can do this. The first is the Müller period (overglaze decoration), when the factory assumed its well-known mark, in 1775, of the three blue lines indicating the three waterways of Denmark—the Sound and the Great and Little Belts. The second great period, the Modern Renaissance (underglaze decoration), practically commenced in 1885.

The porcelain of this factory has long been held in high esteem. Admiral Nelson in 1801, when with the British fleet outside Copenhagen, wrote to Lady Hamilton, "I was in hopes to have got off some Copenhagen china to have sent you"; and later, "As I know you have a valuable collection of china, I send you some of the Copenhagen manufacture." The bowl made at the royal factory in memory of the brave Danes who fell in the battle of Copenhagen is herein illustrated.

The *Encyclopædia Britannica* (11th Edition), 1911 (article on *Ceramics*), awards a high place to the Royal Copenhagen Factory, "the productions of which are not only famous all over the world, but have set a new style in porcelain decoration which is being followed at most of the continental factories."

At the present time museums and private collectors in this country and in various parts of the world are acquiring Royal Copenhagen porcelain on account of its artistic character.

Ordinary collectors of porcelain have always been desirous of selecting a subject which has not been exploited. The Worcester vase which to-day brings two thousand guineas at Christie's was once bought when it was new for as many shillings by some person who recognized its beauty. But in regard to old factories, most of the histories have been written to extol their work when the factory had closed down for ever. The lack of contemporary records of English porcelain is particularly noticeable. It is as though the factories attempted to hide their personalities, as indeed they did disguise their productions by trade signs only decipherable by the indefatigable zeal of later generations. They assumed pseudo-Chinese marks or adopted the crossed L's of Sèvres and the crossed swords of Meissen, to the confusion of collectors a hundred years afterwards. It is therefore with no misgiving that in the present volume modernity receives due consideration. National recognition for the artist potter comes, alas! often too late.

In passing, we may add that there are some wonderful productions being made in England to-day, especially in earthenware, and those who are buying wisely are laying down wine for posterity.

I have to offer my renewed thanks to the various museum authorities, mainly in Scandinavia, and to private collectors and friends who were duly acknowledged in my larger volume as being instrumental in affording me access to data on a new subject.

In that work, although the omission was corrected in the German edition published at Leipsic in 1912, various notes were embodied and remain in the present volume, which were supplied to me by correspondents without any knowledge on my part that they were based on the work of Professor Nyrop of Copenhagen, who has made assiduous research into the history of the old Copenhagen factory, and to whom, therefore, a tribute is in courteous acknowledgment obviously due.

A new chapter has been added to this volume dealing with Copenhagen Art Faience, the character of which ware has claimed recognition from competent critics throughout Europe and in America as having brought a new note into ceramic art.

ARTHUR HAYDEN.

CONTENTS

CHAPTER I

THE EARLY HISTORY OF THE COPENHAGEN FACTORY

THE FOURNIER PERIOD
(1760-1766)

Establishment of porcelain factories in Europe—The German School and the French School—Hard paste—Soft paste—The new ceramic art—The great secret—The secret divulged—The first porcelain in Denmark.

In order to understand the initial stages in the history of the manufacture of porcelain in Denmark, it is necessary to review the peculiar conditions in which china factories existed in the eighteenth century. At the middle of the century there were two great schools, the German and the French. The former made hard or true porcelain according to the formula of Meissen, and the latter made soft or artificial porcelain in the manner of St. Cloud.

Hard Paste.—The impulse of the Western potter had always been to reproduce exactly and chemically the Oriental porcelain. Until the first decade of the eighteenth century this had not been achieved. The news of the great discovery by Johann Fredrich Böttger, in 1709, of a white translucent porcelain, having all the characteristics of the Chinese ware, ran like a flame throughout Europe. Translucent porcelain may be either what is termed hard paste (*pâte dure*), containing only natural elements in the composition of the body and the glaze; or soft paste (*pâte tendre*), where the body is an artificial combination of various materials used as a substitute for the natural earths. All Chinese or true porcelain is of the hard-paste variety. The term *pâte tendre* really applies to the feeble resistance of this artificial porcelain to the action of a high temperature as compared with that offered by true porcelain, and also to the softness of the glaze, which can be scratched by steel.

The body of the true porcelain is essentially of two elements—the white clay or *kaolin*, the infusible element which may be said to be the skeleton, and *petuntse*, the felspathic stone, which is fusible at a high temperature, which may be termed the flesh, and gives transparency to the porcelain. Of the two Chinese names, which have become classical since they were adopted in the dictionary of the French Academy, *kaolin* is the name of a locality where the best porcelain earth is mined, and *petuntse*, literally "white briquettes," refers to the shape in which the finely pulverized porcelain stone is brought to the Chinese potteries, after it has been submitted to the preliminary processes of pounding and decantation.[1]

[1] *Chinese Art*, vol. ii. p. 16, 1906, by Stephen W. Bushell, C.M.G. (late Physician to H.M. Legation, Peking).

Soft Paste.—The artificial porcelain, which was difficult of fabrication, was an imitation of the true Chinese porcelain, although its whiteness, its translucency, and its brilliant glaze have all the appearance of true porcelain. *Kaolin* and *petuntse* are of little importance in the composition of soft porcelain. Its transparency was obtained by the addition of glass, its plasticity by the use of soapstone, and its glaze by an admixture of silica and lead. Moreover, the composition of artificial porcelain has required researches and combinations much more intricate than those which had led to the discovery of hard porcelain, the latter being produced by two substances already provided by nature.

Imitative porcelain had been made at Florence under the auspices of the Grand Duke of Tuscany as early as from 1568 to 1587, of which *fabrique* only about thirty pieces are known. France is the most prolific in porcelain factories of the *pâte tendre*, as it came afterwards to be termed in contradistinction to the *pâte dure* or true porcelain of Meissen. The factory at St. Cloud lasted from 1695 till 1773. Vincennes was founded in 1740, and was finally transferred to Sèvres in 1756, which factory stands paramount in its porcelain, known to collectors as *vieux Sèvres*.

At Nove, near Venice, in 1752, Pasqual Antonibon brought from Meissen a potter, Sigismond Fischer, to construct a furnace for making porcelain in the Saxon style. In 1761 there were three furnaces, one for hard paste *ad uso Sassonia*, and two for soft paste *ad uso Francia*.[2]

[2] *Marks and Monograms on Pottery and Porcelain*, by William Chaffers. (Letter from Francesco Antonibon to Lady Charlotte Schreiber.)

It will thus be seen that the two schools had begun to run side by side. The crowning point was in 1768, when the Sèvres factory commenced to make hard paste. Both bodies were simultaneously made until 1804, after which the manufacture of soft porcelain at Sèvres was discontinued by M. Brongniart. In 1847, the old style was revived by his successor, M. Edelman (*Report on Pottery at the Paris Exhibition by M. Arnoux*, 1867).

In general, it may be said that the manufacture of soft porcelain is beset with difficulties and uncertainties. Its artificial composition renders it capricious in the kiln. In connection therefore with the modern manufacture of Sèvres of the old *pâte tendre* variety, it is interesting to record that in the late eighties the original formulæ of the early potters were used in an attempt to reproduce the old body, but had, after repeated and costly failures, to be abandoned as hopeless.

SUCRIER AND COVER.
Fournier period (1760-1766). Soft-paste porcelain.

DISH AND COVER AND CUSTARD CUP.
Fournier period (1760-1766). Soft-paste porcelain.
(*At Rosenborg Castle, Copenhagen.*)

     In regard to England, it is interesting to note in passing that the old porcelains so highly prized by collectors are all artificial with the exception of Plymouth (1768-1771), Bristol (1771-1781), followed by the company of Staffordshire potters at New Hall who bought the Bristol factory patents, although Wedgwood in his jasper ware and Staffordshire salt glazed ware are fine stone wares which approximate to true porcelain.

     Our soft-paste factories are here set in chronological order: Bow (1745), Chelsea (1745), Derby (1751), Worcester (1751), Lowestoft (1762), Caughley (1772), Pinxton (1795), Coalport (1798), Minton (1798). It should be observed that these, as do all soft-paste porcelains, differ in body in an enormous degree, whereas the true porcelain differs in a minor degree whether it be Canton or Meissen.

It was only for fifty years that the English potters used the capricious body of the glassy soft porcelains then made. Gradually, by experiment, the standard body for artificial porcelain was perfected by the addition of bone-ash, which has been adopted since the late eighteenth century in varying forms by all English potters. It is more related to true porcelain, and is as safe to manufacture as that body, and at a lower heat, but it retains many of the qualities of the soft body. The painted colours melt into the glaze in its final firing and produce that mellow effect so much esteemed by connoisseurs of old porcelain. It is peculiarly English, and stands unique in having technical assets not possessed by any other porcelain. This is something great to record to the honour of the English potter in his mastery of technique.

The New Ceramic Art.—The eighteenth century, in spite of the wars which shook the kingdoms of Europe to their foundations, showed a singular enthusiasm for the art of the potter. A reference to a table of the factory marks of European porcelain of that period will disclose the fact that most of the leading factories were under the auspices of royal or noble patrons whose arms or monograms were incorporated in the mark of the factory.

Kings, princes, electors, grand dukes, and margraves vied with each other in producing rival ware. The St. Petersburg factory had the cipher of the Emperor Paul. At Weesp, in Holland, Count Gronsveldt-Diepenbroek's factory, the works were handed over to the direction of a Protestant pastor. From Vienna with the mark of the Austrian arms, to La Haye with the design of the stork, the symbol of the city; from the arms of the Archbishop of Mayence and the cross and initials of the Prince Bishop of Fulda, to the design of Lille, the *Manufacture Royale de Monseigneur le Dauphin* with the crowned dolphin, a bewildering entanglement of royal marks and patrician ciphers is studded on china, to the confusion of collectors, adding zest to the art of the connoisseur.

The Great Secret.—The actual discovery of the composition of true porcelain by Böttger is interwoven with romance, and the betrayal of the secret processes of its manufacture at Meissen to the leading factories of Europe is a record filled with stirring incidents of the most piquant character. The story of young Böttger, the alchemist and inventor, is told in full by Professor Ernst Zimmermann, Keeper of the Royal Porcelain Collection at Dresden, *Die Erfindung und Frühzeit des Meissner Porzellans*, Berlin, 1908. The search for the philosopher's stone to transmute baser metals into gold had fascinated all chemists. Böttger was credited with more knowledge than he possessed, and he hastily quitted Berlin to avoid the too assiduous attentions of the King of Prussia. For years he wandered in Saxony, and finally claimed protection in 1701 from Frederick Augustus, Elector of Saxony. His life at the laboratory at Meissen, under Ehrenfried Walter von Tschirnhaus, who was a distinguished scientific scholar, was that of a guarded prisoner with a wonderful secret. Tschirnhaus, who was a good chemist, established a glass furnace and invented an ingenious burning mirror, and had essayed to make porcelain. But on the assumption that it was a vitrification, his results only led him to the production of a milky glass. A specimen of this *milch glass* is in the Japanese Palace at Dresden.

When Charles XII of Sweden invaded Saxony, Böttger and his workmen were hurried off to the impregnable fortress of Königstein, where a laboratory was erected. A year later he was back at Meissen conducting experiments and cheerfully exhorting the workmen. In 1709 he produced his true hard porcelain from natural earth obtained from Aue, near Schneeberg.

The most elaborate precautions were taken at Meissen to prevent the secret becoming known. The earth was delivered in sealed casks. It was in vain that an oath was exacted from each workman and written on the walls—"Silence until death" (*Geheim bis ins grab*). The punishment for betrayal was incarceration as a State prisoner in the fortress of Königsberg for life. The terrible silent conditions of the labour produced a longing on the part of the immured workmen to escape. And escape they did.

The Secret divulged.—In 1718, the year previous to Böttger's death Stolzel, the chief workman at Meissen, made his way to Vienna and proceeded to establish, under the direction of a Belgian named Claude Du Pasquier, a manufactory of hard porcelain. The factory was acquired for the State by the Empress Maria Theresa in 1744.

From Vienna a workman named Ringler carried the secret far and wide. His name is linked with the founding of several factories—at Höchst in 1740, at Frankenthal in 1754, where he became director, at Nymphenberg in 1756, where his aid was invoked, at Ludwigsberg (in Würtemberg) in 1758, and at Zurich in 1759.

The workmen of Höchst, in their turn, further divulged the secret. Bengraf, in 1750, carried the process to Fürstenberg, the factory under the patronage of the Duke of Brunswick.

In 1744 an imperial china factory was established at St. Petersburg by the Empress Elizabeth Petrowna, who employed workmen from Meissen, and in 1765, under the patronage of the Empress Catherine II, the works were enlarged.

There were two methods of obtaining the great secret of Meissen—by stealth and by experiment; most of the factories employed the former means. The attempts to arrive at the hard paste by experiment resulted in the establishment of many soft-paste factories. One remarkable instance of indefatigable industry is that of the chemist Pott, in the employ of the King of Prussia at Berlin, who endeavoured honestly to arrive at the nature of the composition of the Meissen body. He is credited with having made no fewer than thirty thousand experiments, and in so doing he contributed largely to the modern chemical knowledge of the effect of high temperatures on minerals.[3]

[3] Roscoe and Schorlemmer, *Treatise on Chemistry*, vol. ii. p. 598.

It is thus seen how great was the discovery of Böttger, of Meissen, and how far-reaching were the results of the manufacture of true porcelain in Saxony. A wild burst of enthusiasm followed which has been rarely equalled. Soldier-princes engaged in the wars which were waged in the German States turned aside to indulge in speculation concerning the new art. In 1717 about a hundred and fifty pieces of fine porcelain, many of them old Oriental, now at the Japanese Palace at Dresden, were acquired by Augustus the Strong of Saxony from the King of Prussia in exchange for a regiment of dragoons, without uniforms, horses, or arms.

When the vigilant Frederick the Great commenced the Seven Years' War, and on a sudden filled the electorate of Saxony with sixty thousand Prussian troops, Dresden was taken. It was in vain that the Queen of Poland, daughter of an emperor and mother-in-law of a dauphin, placed the secret State documents in her bedroom to avoid seizure. They were too valuable to Frederick, who had them forcibly removed, and by publishing them proved that he was to be assailed at once by Austria, France, Russia, Sweden, Saxony, and the Germanic body.

The factory of Meissen was depleted of material and models, and he transported artists and workmen to Berlin to found his factory there. Five hundred persons were engaged at this new factory, and in order to win commercial success he executed a master-stroke by framing a decree that all Jews in his kingdom must produce a voucher from the director of the factory that they had purchased a certain amount of the royal porcelain before permission would be granted to enable them to marry.

VASE (ONE OF A PAIR).
Decorated in rococo style with panels having allegorical subjects, one of which has a medallion supported by cupids upon which a crown and F5 are inscribed in gold. Festoons of flowers, painted in natural colours, are suspended from a ring at top of vase; all in high relief. Marked F5 in gold.
*(**In the collection of Count Moltke, of Bregentved.**)*

It is such human touches as these, significant in their piquancy, which give exceptional interest to the porcelain of the old days produced in conditions of no little difficulty. Under Court patronage, beset by espionage and hedged about by intrigue, the secret of one factory rapidly found its way across the frontier to the neighbouring State. The fortunes of potters have not lain in smooth places, and fate has been as capricious as the fire of the furnace. In eighteenth-century days the *furore* of mad dilettantism pursued them relentlessly. Royal amateurs more often than not asked them to make bricks without straw, and there was still in the air the lingering suspicion that the furnace might yield up the secret of the philosopher's stone and fill the State treasury to the full.

The First Porcelain in Denmark.—It is not difficult to imagine the situation.

9

King Frederik V determined to found a porcelain factory of his own. His queen consort was Louise, daughter of George II, who died in 1751, eight years after her marriage. His second wife was Juliane Marie, of Brunswick-Wolfenbüttel.

Mark.
       Fournier period (1760-1766).
Soft-paste Porcelain.

Faience was made at various factories in Denmark, and it is more than conjectural that various native attempts were made to produce porcelain. The royal factory, which the king built near the Blue Tower at Christianshavn, with the aid of foreign workmen whom he had induced to enter his service, commenced to make various experiments. Mehlhorn was one of the alien potters brought from Saxony, but apparently, whether from paucity of natural earths or owing to faulty kilns, nothing of any moment resulted until Louis Fournier, a Frenchman (1760-1766), was induced to take charge of the factory. During what is known as the Fournier period the French director had the assistance of Danish artists, including Johannes Wiedewelt the sculptor. His contemporaries speak of the services he designed. Doubtless many of them were intended as presents to foreign princes and ambassadors, and found their way into royal and foreign cabinets. Although only about twenty pieces of the Fournier period are known, it is not impossible that careful research may discover that some of the early pieces attributed to Fürstenberg may really belong to Fournier of Copenhagen. Obviously, on account of their rarity they are of great value and of exceptional interest as being the first creations of the Royal Copenhagen Porcelain Factory. The identification should be rendered the easier when it is borne in mind that the early Copenhagen porcelain of the Fournier period is soft paste, whereas the Fürstenberg porcelain is hard paste. The mark F with the figure 5 stands for Frederik V and not for Fournier. The coincidence of the initial letter is like the W in Worcester porcelain of the Dr. Wall period.

The early creations of the Copenhagen factory were porcelain, it is true, but they are not the hard or true porcelain of Meissen. They are the soft paste of the same nature as the *pâte tendre* of contemporary Sèvres. They did not attain the high ideal contemplated by Frederik V when he set out to equal the Saxon porcelain and the other hard-paste porcelains of Germany, but they arrived at a dignity and a grace of style which are worthy of regard. As first attempts they are of surprising beauty, and the few specimens remaining arouse curiosity as to what masterpieces of this short period have been lost to posterity.

The modelling, the design, and the colouring of such early examples as these of a new factory are naturally dependent on prototypes. It was a great thing to produce porcelain at all, consequently the style is found to be derivative. A fine Sèvres jar with cover, in date 1761, at the Sèvres Museum, has a family likeness to the Fournier cups with covers in Rosenborg Castle, Copenhagen. Although these latter have the same type of decoration with a white panel on a dark ground, it will be seen that the Sèvres example exhibits the sure mastery of technique of an older factory. The painting is richer and of more detail, with birds of tropical plumage. The Fournier examples, with handles, were evidently designed for use. There are five of these covered custard cups at Rosenborg Castle, three having green and two having blue grounds; we illustrate an example. At the *Kunstindustri Museum* at Copenhagen there are two custard cups and covers of similar form—one with red decoration; and the other with red and green, and floral decoration painted in colours. These are both marked F5 in blue.

It is interesting to note, in the archives of the Sèvres factory, that Louis XV sent, in 1758, to the King of Denmark a service of green, decorated with figures, flowers, and birds, which cost 30,000 livres. Here, at hand, was a fine Sèvres service as model for Fournier, and the resemblance of soft-paste Copenhagen porcelain to Sèvres is not difficult to understand.

In the illustration of the *Oval Dish and Cover* standing beside the cup with handle, the ware is coarser and in paste and colouring is not unlike some of the earlier specimens of Bow china. These and the other illustration of *Sucrier with Cover and Dish* are from the famous collection at Rosenborg Castle. The sucrier and cover are decorated with scale pattern; portions of the outer rim are moulded in relief and the floral decoration is in natural colours.

A *Teapot* from a tea service at the National Museum at Stockholm exhibits a similar style in this experimental period. The colours of the teapot, cream jug, and cups and saucers are emerald green borders with gilding. The flowers are painted in natural colours. They bear the Fournier mark F5 in gold. The service was a present to King Charles XV of Sweden from the Countess Dannemand.

In the collection of Count Moltke of Bregentved are four fine *Vases* of this period. They exhibit the rococo style then prevalent and are remarkable works emanating from the little royal factory of Copenhagen during the first years of its existence. On one of these vases is a panel decorated with a group of Cupids supporting a shield upon which is inscribed the mark used by Fournier in the period of Frederik V.

All these soft-paste Copenhagen examples are of great rarity. The Fournier period was of short duration. The death of Frederik V, in 1766, removed its royal patron. The winter of 1766-7 brought great distress in Copenhagen, and the masked balls and masquerades and the luxurious riot of the Court of the young king Christian VII at Christianborg inflamed public opinion against the new monarch.

It is obvious that at such a juncture the royal factory, which in its struggling infancy needed enthusiastic patronage, suffered from neglect so that it is not surprising to find that its days were numbered, and after a vain struggle it finally ceased work. Louis Fournier returned to France, and the first period of Copenhagen porcelain came to an end.

CHAPTER II

FRANTZ HEINRICH MÜLLER
(1773-1801)

QUEEN JULIANE MARIE PERIOD
PART I (1775-1780)

PORTRAIT OF FRANTZ HEINRICH MÜLLER.
(From an old lithograph.)
Reproduced by kind permission of "Tidsskrift for Industri," Copenhagen.

CHRONOLOGY

1732. Frantz Heinrich Müller born, 17th November.

1765. Müller solicits support for the establishment of a porcelain factory.

1773. Frantz Heinrich Müller presents his first pieces of hard-fired transparent porcelain to Christian VII. The first hard porcelain made in Denmark.

1775. A company formed, of which the members of the Royal Family held shares. The Dowager Queen Juliane Marie suggests the factory mark of the three blue lines, symbolizing the three waterways of Denmark, which mark was adopted and has been continuously used since that date.

1779. The factory taken over by the king becomes the Royal Porcelain Manufactory.

1780. The first retail depot opened in Copenhagen.

CHAPTER II

FRANTZ HEINRICH MÜLLER
(1773-1801)

QUEEN JULIANE MARIE PERIOD
Part I (1775-1780)

The Court of the young king Christian VII—A great Court scandal—A *Coup d'Etat*—The inception of the Porcelain Factory—The origin of the mark of the Three Blue Lines—Müller's technique—Müller's range of subjects.

At the death of King Frederik V, in January 1766, and the succession of Christian VII, then seventeen years of age, the royal china factory at the Blue Tower fell upon evil days. When Frantz Heinrich Müller, "only after numerous unsuccessful attempts," presented his first three pieces of hard-fired transparent porcelain to the young king in September 1773, there were matters of much graver moment occupying public attention. It was almost in vain that Müller had built new kilns differing from those in which soft porcelain was made, travelled to Bornholm to find suitable clay, and experimented with glazes.

In the six years since the death of Frederik, Denmark had passed through one of the most tragical periods of her history. Christian VII, a manikin prince, became the sport of fate. Caroline Matilda, the sister of George III of England, at the early age of fifteen, became his queen. Himself the son of the beloved Louise, daughter of George II, great hopes were entertained by the Danish people of the alliance. But perverse circumstances —with the grim figure of the Dowager Queen Juliane Marie in the background—beset the path of the young couple.

The Court at Christianborg, an echo of Versailles, filled with painted men and women who affected to despise Danish customs and even the Danish tongue, was a hot-bed of intrigue. Christian threw etiquette to the winds in his sanctum, surrounded by boon companions. The coterie had all the abandon of Sans Souci without the master-mind of Frederick of Prussia and the wit and satire of that monarch's *confidantes*. Madame de Plessen, lady-in-waiting, stern precisian in etiquette, devoted to her young mistress, but heedlessly tactless, made a breach between the king and queen. The bride of a year retired to the company of staid dowagers and played chess. The petulance and malicious tricks of the king early showed that, unable to govern himself, he was unable to govern others. Madame de Plessen was dismissed by the king and ordered to leave Denmark. Christian's dissipation was rapidly becoming a public scandal. The "Northern Rogue" was the mild epithet of the English populace, who cheered the little king when he came to St. James's. Echoes of his wild life reached Matilda at Copenhagen.

VASE WITH COVER.
With wreaths of roses and other flowers in high relief, painted in natural colours. Cover with seated figure of cupid with garland. Panel with painted portrait of the Dowager Queen Juliane Marie. Height 15 inches.
(*At Rosenborg Castle, Copenhagen.*)

A Great Court Scandal.—At this juncture a remarkable man, John Frederick Struensee, the king's physician, a German, possessed of extraordinary talents, gradually began to assume control of State affairs. The tragic story is too intricate to refer to here in more than a cursory manner. Queen Matilda's attachment to Struensee is as romantic as that of Mary Queen of Scots for Rizzio. An English author has termed her "A Queen of Tears."[4] It is Madame de Genlis who affirms that "men summon physicians only when they suffer, women when they are merely afflicted with *ennui*." In six years this man became the most powerful in Denmark. An amazing state of things followed. The envoys of the various Powers became alarmed at the situation. Drastic reforms followed one another in quick succession, inaugurated by Struensee, but promulgated in the king's name. Undoubtedly Struensee had a genius for government had he tempered his reforms with discretion. He was saturated with German philosophy, and based his ethics on Voltaire and the sordid sentiment of Rousseau. "It is the path of the passions that has conducted me to philosophy," writes Jean-Jacques, and Struensee might well have applauded that sentiment. He invented a new office and became "Master of Requests" and virtually Prime Minister. But he offended too many people's interests and became the object of hatred. He galled the old nobility by his despotic power, and the Dowager-Queen Juliane Marie, from her seclusion at Fredensborg, filled the Court with spies. The weak-minded king, now showing signs of mental aberration, signed everything put before him, and the young Queen Matilda was under the domination of Struensee, who openly treated her with disrespect.

[4] *A Queen of Tears, Caroline Matilda, Queen of Denmark and Norway, and Princess of Great Britain and Ireland*, by W. H. Wilkins, M.A., F.S.A. (2 vols.), London, 1904.

In 1771 there was great distress in the country and discontent was growing. Scurrilous letters fell at the feet of Struensee and Matilda on their walks at Hirscholm, and placards of a threatening nature were affixed to the walls of the royal palaces. Struensee had flouted the army by attempting to disband the Guards. The mutterings of disaffection became more audible. His effrontery deserted him. He grew craven-hearted in face of grave dangers. His failure stamps him as a colossal adventurer at bottom; had he been of sterner stuff he might have become a hero.

A Coup d'Etat.—The hour for striking a blow was at hand, and Queen Juliane Marie and her son Frederik, with a band of conspirators, at a masked ball on the night of January 16, 1772, seized the person of the king, together with Matilda; the latter was hurried off to the fortress of Kronborg, and Struensee and Brandt, his coadjutor, were imprisoned in the citadel at Copenhagen.

VASE WITH COVER.
    With wreaths of roses and other flowers in high relief, painted in natural colours. Cover with seated figure of cupid with garland Panel with painted portrait of the Crown Prince Frederik. Height 15 inches.
    (*At Rosenborg Castle, Copenhagen.*)

The trial and divorce of Matilda and the beheading of Struensee and Brandt is a poignant story. The name of the unfortunate young queen was ordered to be officially omitted from the prayer-book at a time when she surely stood most in need of prayer. Juliane Marie pursued Matilda with vindictiveness, and her malevolence nearly precipitated Denmark in a war with England. It was intended that Matilda should be imprisoned in a remote fortress in Jutland. The British Minister, Sir Robert Murray Keith, informed the Danish Government that unless Queen Matilda was released he would present his letters of recall and war would be declared. The Danish Minister in London wrote in great haste to say that a fleet was fitting out. It was only then that Queen Juliane Marie released her hold of Matilda and allowed her to depart to Celle, in the State of Hanover, where she died in 1775 in her twenty-third year.

Here, then, was the state of affairs when Müller was experimenting with his clays, his glazes, and his colours. In 1771 a hundred and fifty weavers set out on foot from Copenhagen to Hirscholm, in days of panic, to complain that they were starving because the royal silk factory was closed. It was an ill-starred venture to attempt the establishment of a new porcelain factory, but in face of reverses of fortune and undeterred by lack of support, Müller by his immense energy fired into being the great porcelain factory of Copenhagen. To Müller the Dane belongs the honour of founding the little factory which strove to achieve results no less beautiful than Meissen, Berlin, or Sèvres. Begun in a spirit of worthy emulation, the Copenhagen factory shortly began to develop an original and national style, in spite of the fact that it worked in the early days on foreign suggestion and employed foreign artists.

The Inception of the Porcelain Factory.—Frantz Heinrich Müller was born on the 17th of November 1732. When an apprentice, from the age of fifteen, at the Kong Salomon's Pharmacy at Copenhagen, he devoted his leisure to the study of chemistry, botany, mineralogy, and metallurgy. He was appointed as Guardian of the Mint at the Bank of Copenhagen in his twenty-eighth year, and held the post from 1760 to 1767. As early as 1765 he had the object in view of establishing a porcelain factory; together with a painter named Richter we find him soliciting support. In common with his contemporaries he cast eager eyes on foreign porcelain. He wandered for three years on the Continent under an assumed name, and the unravelling of this period of his career would throw much light on his researches.

PORTION OF TEA AND COFFEE SERVICE, WITH TEA-CADDIES, ETC.
Decorated, overglaze, in Indian red.

Müller, on his secret mission in Germany, found that the china factories of Fürstenberg, Meissen, and Berlin were closed to him. But he threw his whole life and energy into his work. He outlived the opposition of the Society of Apothecaries, who objected to a licence being granted him as a druggist and dispenser. But in face of the objection the College of Medicine found the applicant "a very capable, learned, and experienced man, not only in Pharmacy, but also in Chemistry, Assaying, and Natural History." With characteristic energy he passed the pharmaceutical examination at the age of forty-one; already he had shown originality and inventiveness by making several discoveries in colours and in dyeing. But with all his virility he found financial success no easy matter at such a disturbed period. He endeavoured to form a company for the manufacture of Danish porcelain. To his chagrin, only one share was sold.

At the outset there was little promise that his untiring efforts would win the remotest recognition from his countrymen. It seemed imminent that the whole enterprise would have to be abandoned. Happily, Privy Chancellor Holm, the private secretary to the Dowager-Queen Juliane Marie, saw possibilities in the venture. To revive the old factory which Fournier had vacated was an opportunity not to be missed. If it proved a success, it would redound to the credit of the queen and add lustre to the new *régime* just commenced under the sway of Juliane Marie, with Guldberg as the power behind the throne. Christian VII had simply passed as a signer of documents into the keeping of another set of masters.

Of the shares, most of them in the new factory were held by members of the royal family and one by Müller himself. The directors were Holm; Suhm, the historian; General Eickstedt, one of the conspirators who took a leading part in the arrest at the masked ball; and Guldberg, who had a finger in every pie. On the 13th of March 1775 the company obtained the monopoly of the manufacture of porcelain in all the dominions of the King of Denmark, in spite of the opposition of the Board of Trade.

The Origin of the Mark of the Three Blue Lines.—The first meeting of the company was held on the 1st of May 1775. It was decided that the trade-mark of the factory, according to the proposal of Queen Juliane Marie, should be three wavy lines, always marked in blue, representing Denmark's three waterways—*Oresund*, and the two belts: *Storebelt*, between Sjaelland and Fyen; *Lillebelt*, between Fyen and Jutland. With this trade-mark of the three blue lines the Copenhagen factory (*Den Danske Porcellænsfabrik*) took its place beside the older factories on the Continent, and to this day, a hundred and forty-three years afterwards, this same mark appears on all porcelain emanating from the Royal Copenhagen Factory.

SAUCER.
Subject, Eagle and lamb painted in natural colours. Richly gilded border.
(At the Kunstindustri Museum, Copenhagen.)

Although Müller only had one share of the subscribed capital, there was only one controlling brain. He worked the enterprise single-handedly. It was "*par ses seules lumières,*" to quote a contemporary French account of the factory, that he had succeeded in producing the beautiful porcelain which won early recognition from connoisseurs. But the Court were not eager to encourage ambition. After the late startling exhibition of a now defunct medico, whose head still stuck on a pole on Gallows Hill, genius must needs be rigorously safeguarded. In common, therefore, with his artisans, Müller was required to sign a contract binding him to remain in the employ of the Court factory, and to keep secret all that he knew of the manufacture of porcelain—his own invention. His official position was only that of works manager.

Genius, that indomitable and unquenchable spirit which overrides all obstacles, found Müller, with his crowd of untried soldier workmen and crude apprentices, ceaselessly working in the factory from five in the morning till seven in the evening, and often superintending the firing all night. In 1776 three workmen were inveigled from Meissen to the Court factory at Copenhagen, but only two out of the three showed any ability. Their supercilious manners, together with their higher wages, brought trouble in the factory among the other workmen, and Müller expelled them by force. But he made one appointment which undoubtedly was of benefit to the factory; by contributing part of the salary himself, he brought A. C. Luplau from the Fürstenberg factory, who became modelling master. As early as 1776 the name of Baÿer appears as a painter in colours, as opposed to the painters in underglaze blue. It was Baÿer who afterwards was entrusted with the painting of the celebrated *Flora Danica* service, begun in 1790. Others whose names are found in the early records are Hans Clio and the portrait painters, Camrath and Ondrup.

The first four years of the factory were very critical. Notwithstanding the close application of Müller, the financial position came to a serious crisis in 1779. There seemed every likelihood that the factory would follow in the steps of Fournier and close its doors. How the royal shareholders adjusted matters is not known, nor what became of Müller's one share in the enterprise. The debts were paid in the king's name, and the factory was taken over by the State and became the Royal Porcelain Manufactory (*Den Kongelige Porcellænsfabrik*), which name it bears at the present day. In March 1780 a retail business was opened at Copenhagen in connection with the factory. Müller was made inspector of the factory and the title of Councillor of Justice was conferred upon him.

SAUCER.
     Subject, Water-god painted in purple, with green wreath of aquatic foliage on a base of shells and seaweed.
     (At the Kunstindustri Museum, Copenhagen.)

Dated specimens have an exceptional interest in proving that no inconsiderable progress had at that time been made in the artistic development of the factory. Already in form and in decoration there was something distinctive in Müller's ware. Such pieces show indisputably that great days were at hand, if indeed in these first few years success had not already been achieved in training artists and craftsmen in the new industry.

Müller's Technique.—Danish ceramic art is profoundly indebted to Müller for his pioneer work. He was a giant in days when pigmies controlled the destinies. His unflagging energy, his practical experiments, and his original and inventive genius impelled him to implant national characteristics in the Royal Copenhagen porcelain which have never departed from the ware of this factory. His first attempts were made with kaolin which he obtained from the island of Bornholm. He soon realized that this did not fulfil all the conditions necessary for a fine body. It was of a greyish-blue tint, and was liable to lose its shape in firing. In appearance it is not very transparent and is somewhat coarse, like some of the old Japanese porcelain. Of this Bornholm period mention will be made later in dealing with the early examples of blue underglaze painted ware, which is a special variety by itself, running concurrently with the overglaze painted ware which Müller brought in his best period to unexampled perfection.

He prepared the glazes himself, determined the correct method of firing, and made the colours used at the factory. The blue that he invented is perfect, and is to be found on the early specimens of underglaze painted porcelain for domestic use. The green and the purple found in the early Müller period were his own discovery and of exceptional quality in tone. He was a master of technique, and perfected a new body which he called "virgin paste." This is of a dazzling white, and Müller's glaze is transparent and smooth as polished crystal. The tint is that of the green of the sea, and without doubt its technical excellence lends great beauty to the porcelain of this period. Considering the primitive methods of working and the impure materials then available, the perfection and beauty of the results claim profound admiration from the connoisseur. Even with the aid of modern technology and chemistry it has not yet been found possible to equal the technique of Müller's best period.

The year 1780, the date when the first opening of the retail business took place, was the turning-point in the history of the factory. Müller was acclaimed as a genius by his countrymen. It was proposed that a statue should be erected to his honour—and this in his lifetime. A wave of enthusiasm found an outlet in Latin poems to "the man who had done so much for his king and country." It is exceptional to find such contemporary honour bestowed on a potter. Rarely is a man a prophet in his own country. But happily Müller lived to wear the laurel wreath. "What honour," writes a contemporary, "this industry has brought its founder! I was enraptured with the things which I saw. How could I have dreamed that these could be made by a Dane and in my native land!"

COFFEE CUPS.
Painted in overglaze colours with blue border richly gilded.
Rose and spray in natural colours.
Group of cavalry in rich uniform, in colours.

We catch an insight into Müller's methods from a letter he wrote, when eighty years of age, to Boye, a subsequent director, who had suggested the use of some pieces of new apparatus for the laboratory. Old Müller wrote as follows: "I fail to see the use or necessity of the thermometer, eudiometer, or hydrometer. I have never found it necessary to apply such exact learning in the manufacture of porcelain, and ideas such as these appear to me to be absolutely absurd." While allowance must be made for Müller's advanced age and his hypersensitiveness towards his successors, it is of great interest to speculate upon his point of view. Man of science that he was, his deprecatory regard for these instruments seems to denote that his technique was arrived at by practical rule-ofthumb methods, dependent upon personal exactitude rather than upon formulæ. It is idle to scoff at Müller's conservatism, for science has yet to unravel the secret of the lost art of tempering the Damascene blade and the subtleties of the potter's art of the K'ang Hsi period in the single coloured glazes, *la qualité maîtresse de la céramique*, the delicacies of the rare *peau de pêche*, the *famille rose*, and the *famille verte*. In the late seventeenth and early eighteenth-century days the methods of Chinese potters were as unscientific as those defended by Müller, but the results are "not of an age, but for all time." And Müller's results stand the test of intense criticism; they are hitherto inimitable.

Müller's Range of Subjects.—In regard to the periods of the various styles of Müller, with very few data to guide the critic it must be largely a matter of conjecture as to the exact chronological order of their manufacture. It seems to the present writer, in endeavouring to classify the examples, that they naturally fall under the following heads. One class overlaps another in point of time, and although at first, in the experimental period, elaborate artistic creations cannot at that stage have been attempted, it must equally follow that in the middle and later period the simpler and utilitarian forms were still being made concurrently with the finer works of art.

The natural order of development in point of technique would be:—

Underglaze painted "mussel" blue-and-white fluted porcelain (pp. 161, 163, 167).

Early examples painted in colours overglaze. (See illustrations, pp. 65, 89.) (a) Dishes, plates, tea and coffee services. (b) Vases and ornamental pieces of a minor character.

Vases with modelled figures. Figure subjects in colours.

Busts, in biscuit.

Elaborate and finely modelled vases and sumptuous services, of which the *Flora Danica* is the culmination.

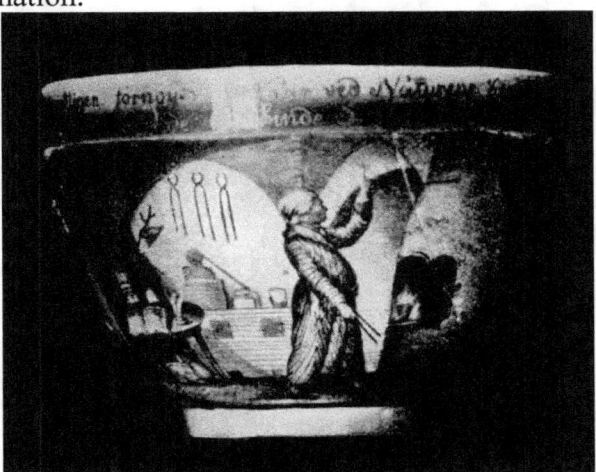

COFFEE CUP.
With painted subject of Frantz Heinrich Müller in his laboratory, in an oval surrounded by wreath of flowers in gold. Marked with three blue lines. Blue border with inscription in verse in gold:—
Forstanden, Sind og Sands kan samtligen förnojes—Naar ved Naturens Kraft paa chymiske veije plöijes—Men vil og Nytten sees da skal Forstanden raade —Og binde Sind om Sands til det som Skatter baade.
(Translation.)
The finest senses may well pleased be—When Nature leans on Science for her aid—

But Art in wedlock with Utility—Demands from skill a double debt be paid.
(At the National Museum, Stockholm.)

It is obvious that in the immature years of a pottery figure subjects would be rarely attempted until such time as the potters were sure of their ground and the technique had been securely established. The highest artistic achievements must necessarily come after the rudiments of the art have been mastered. In regard to figure subjects, the fact that Luplau came to Copenhagen in 1776 with eighteen years' experience from the Fürstenberg factory must be taken into consideration in regard to the appearance, at an earlier stage than usual in the history of a factory, of figures of excellent character. But at the same time it must be borne in mind that the utilitarian blue-and-white services, the national Danish pattern now so well known, were made simultaneously with such fine creations as the elaborate royal services at Rosenborg Castle and elsewhere.

All through the periods from Müller onwards the famous blue-and-white has remained as a standard output; but as a rough generalization, with the reservation admitted in regard to figures, it may be said that the classes above mentioned followed one another in quick succession, until the climax of the Müller period was reached, when the Royal Copenhagen Factory worthily claimed a place beside the great factories in Europe.

CHAPTER III

FRANTZ HEINRICH MÜLLER
(1773-1801) *continued*

QUEEN JULIANE MARIE PERIOD
PART II (1780-1796)

CHRONOLOGY

1780. The first retail depot opened by the Royal Porcelain Manufactory in Copenhagen. The china becomes national.

1784. Queen Juliane Marie and her son Frederik, the Hereditary Prince, overthrown.

The Crown Prince Frederik undertakes the government of the country on behalf of his imbecile father, Christian VII.

1790. The importation of foreign porcelain into Denmark prohibited.

The great *Flora Danica* service for Catherine II, Empress of Russia, commenced.

1796. Queen Juliane Marie dies in retirement.

1801. The battle of Copenhagen.

Müller retires from active work at the factory, then in his sixty-ninth year.

1807. Copenhagen bombarded by the British fleet. Considerable damage done to the Royal Porcelain Factory.

1808. The Crown Prince Frederik ascends the throne as Frederik VI on the death of his father, Christian VII.

The *Flora Danica* service completed.

1820. Death of Müller. Buried 9th March.

CHAPTER III

FRANTZ HEINRICH MÜLLER
(1773-1801) *continued*

QUEEN JULIANE MARIE PERIOD
Part II (1780-1796)

The great outburst of activity in 1780—The manufacture of porcelain an assured success—A contemporary account of the factory—A national style created—The diversity of Müller's designs—National sentiment—Table of marks (1775-1801)—List of leading painters and modellers (1773-1801).

The masterpieces of Müller come, as do all *chefs-d'œuvres*, as a surprise. Their gracefulness and poetic charm are captivating. To those who have never had the opportunity to examine a fine collection of old Copenhagen porcelain the discovery of these works of art is a revelation. It has hitherto been supposed that the productions of the little Danish factory were only imitative of the works of the older and better-known German factories. But to the most superficial observer it is at once evident that here is something at once national and beautiful.

During the ten years subsequent to the opening of the retail establishment in Copenhagen, the output of the factory must have been very extensive. It is interesting to find that in 1790 the Custom House regulations relative to the subject are as follows: "Foreign china is prohibited, because the manufactory at Copenhagen, which is at the charge of the State, has been of late productive enough to supply the two kingdoms with an article of luxury, more than of necessity. Painted earthenware is likewise prohibited, from its resemblance to china being so great that many may be induced to purchase it instead of a more valuable article; but plain earthenware, being more generally necessary, is allowed, as is also the porcelain brought over by the East India ships belonging to the Asiatic Company."

A Contemporary Account of the Factory.—The testimony of two foreign critics who visited the factory in 1790 is a valuable record, as they produced authoritative statistical volumes on Northern Europe. Their opinion assists the modern student in forming an estimate of the relative value of the Royal Copenhagen porcelain as compared with that of the great contemporary factories, especially Meissen. In *Les Voyages de deux François dans le Nord de l'Europe* (the Chevalier Louis de Boisgelin and the Comte

Alfonse de Fortia), published by the latter, the trade and manufactures of Denmark receive full treatment.

We quote from the English edition, *Travels through Denmark and Sweden: to which is prefixed a Journal of a Voyage down the Elbe from Dresden to Hamburgh, including a compendious historical account of the Hanseatic League, by Louis de Boisgelin, Knight of Malta, with views from drawings taken on the spot by Dr. Charles Parry*. This was published in two quarto volumes in 1810. The author states that the former volume written by his fellow-traveller is so rare that it is hardly possible to procure a copy "either of the original edition or of the counterfeit one produced in Germany."

The details in regard to the factory as it then existed are very interesting. There were three large and two small ovens; one of these was the first employed by Müller when he produced his hard porcelain. The ovens were of brick. A firing lasted eighteen hours. It took four days to cool. "These ovens are capable of firing eight complete services at once, whereas those of Saxony cannot take in more than three. The fire here is so well distributed that in many of the firings of fine porcelain the loss sustained is scarcely more than ten rix-dollars."

After describing the process of glazing, the writer proceeds to describe the most important operation of all, performed in a room "where there is only one man, who takes an oath to have no communication whatsoever with any other workman. He works a mill by hand in which he prepares the paste, and mixes the different matters which compose the glaze." Of the mills for grinding there were two. The granite came from Zealand; "the black is of no use for this operation, which is not performed in the same manner as in Saxony, where the matter is mixed without water, but here it is quite the contrary. By the method employed in this country there is as much made in two hours as they can possibly produce in Saxony in twenty-four; besides the advantage of having no occasion for sieves."

A contemporary account such as this by competent observers who had visited other porcelain factories in Europe and came with the definite object of finding out as much as possible, is of supreme importance as a document. It appears that the blue which came from Norway was considered the finest. There was an immense loft for "coffins," or cases, to be stored for a year before being ready for use. These were made from Bornholm clay, and were used in the ovens as "saggers," as the term is in English pottery, to contain the porcelain. "The moulds are made of a kind of plaster which comes from France. This," says the narrative, "is the only foreign article employed in the manufactory."

In regard to the overglaze colours used there are some interesting facts. Yellow is made from pure tin; purple, with tin and gold; dark poppy, with iron; sky-blue, with cobalt; black, with manganese; rose-colour, with gold; and green, with copper. "These colours never change in firing, but remain precisely as they were first drawn; whereas they spread in many other factories."

Bearing in mind that the travellers were comparing the manufactures of one country with another in their precise records, which excited European interest in regard to their statistic and economic value, the praise of the Royal Copenhagen porcelain makes the more pleasant reading. "The Copenhagen porcelain is less glassy than that of China.

The paste of the biscuit is lighter and closer than that of the Saxon porcelain, the white keeps its colour better, and it is easier to wash. In short, the whole of this manufacture is perfectly well understood, and carried on with great spirit and diligence. It has only been established thirteen years, and at the end of four the storehouses were already filled with a variety of articles. We saw some flutes, for which they asked seventy rix-dollars each. These are very just in tune, but too heavy to be played upon conveniently; they are likewise astonishingly brittle. We were also shown vases two and a half feet high most beautifully painted by Camrath."

The writer makes one extraordinary statement, which goes to show that the finest works were made for rich people, and were not seen by the Danish people in general. "The Copenhagen porcelain is very little known even in Denmark; for the original expenses of a manufacture of this nature are such, that it must necessarily be sold very dear: it is indeed more so at present than the Saxon china; but it is imagined the price will be lowered in a short time."

The number of workmen employed at the factory at the time of this inspection was three hundred, "forty of whom were for the painting part of the business, which we thought but few for that important branch."

In regard to the director, Müller, himself, some trenchant criticisms are made as to the poor recognition the State had given to so great a potter. In other factories there were different directors, one for the body and glaze, another for the ovens and firing, a third for the artistic form, and a fourth for the painting and gilding, all of whom were paid at a high rate. "But here M. Müller, an excellent chemist, acts himself in these various departments, and is very shabbily paid, having only a salary of 500 rix-dollars. He is also the original inventor of this manufacture, and when it is known that he was never out of Copenhagen, and consequently could have had no model to go by, it is inconceivable to what a degree of perfection he has brought it, and that, too, entirely from his own enlightened genius, without the smallest foreign assistance."

SUCRIER WITH COVER, AND CUP.
With deep-blue bands having rich and elaborate gilding. *Sucrier* with panel inscribed *Guds Frücht*, figure representing Harvest. Cup with convolvulus painted in natural colours.
(*At Dansk Folke Museum, Copenhagen.*)

Concerning the salary of Müller of 500 rix-dollars per annum, it is noteworthy to observe that at that time the retail price in Copenhagen of a complete afternoon service, consisting of six chocolate cups with handles, twelve coffee cups, coffee-pot, teapot and dish, sugar dish, tea caddy and cream jug, was 19 rix-dollars 3 marks first quality blue-and-white, and 26 rix-dollars 4 marks painted with natural flowers. Müller's yearly labours were evidently reckoned as only worth a score of such afternoon services. Hence the piquant strictures of the foreign noblemen.

The point raised as to Müller not having had the smallest foreign assistance may be dismissed as somewhat erroneous. There was Anton Carl Luplau, who was at the Fürstenberg factory for eighteen years, and who came to Copenhagen in 1776; Johan Christoph Baÿer, who was born in Nuremberg, and came to Copenhagen in 1768, when he was thirty years old; Peter Heinrich Benjamin Lehmann, who was a native of Hamburg, and came to Copenhagen from the Berlin factory in 1780, and was naturalized in 1781; Carl Fridrich Thomaschefsky, who worked a short time at the factory; and Martin Cadewitz, who served eleven years and died in 1791. But in 1781, of two hundred persons employed at the factory only ten were foreigners.

As to whether Müller ever left Copenhagen the Count de Boisgelin adds a footnote: "According to M. Catteau, this was not the fact; we only repeat what the man told us was the case." The work referred to is *Le Tableau des Etats Dannois envisagés sous le Rapport du Mécanisme Social, par Jean Pierre Catteau*, printed in Paris in 1802 in three volumes.

It is rather an interesting point, but the evidence is against de Boisgelin, for Müller not only visited Brunswick when he entered into negotiations with Luplau to enter the Danish service, but at a slightly earlier date he made a tour of the German factories— in an assumed name, as some accounts go. That he made good use of his time is amply borne out by the results he achieved in so short a space of time on his return to his native land.

There is nothing to detract from the originality and inventiveness of his work. The personality of his genius illuminates the work of the factory. He experienced as many reverses of fortune as did Bernard Palissy, and battled against adverse circumstances with no less indomitable spirit. He conquered technical difficulties, and experimented with clays and bodies and glazes and pigments with hardly less assiduity than did Josiah Wedgwood.

A National Style Created.—No art is wholly independent in origin or of sporadic growth. In the early days and the initial stages it must always be derivative. In ceramic art this applies either to form or decoration, often to both. The form and decoration of Chinese blue-and-white porcelain was the basis of the school of Delft faience. The scale pattern and the panel with exotic birds were slavishly adopted at Sèvres from Oriental prototypes. Similarly the older European factories impressed their styles upon factories of a later growth. The crowd of German factories came under the direct influence of Meissen in design as well as in technique. It is a significant fact that Copenhagen porcelain under Müller's guiding spirit developed an original style from the first establishment of the factory. This achievement should be placed to Müller's credit in determining his position among European potters. He did something more than assimilate the technique of Meissen in his hard paste, and the fact that he was the first man to make real porcelain in Denmark is only a part of the honour due to him. He created what was far more difficult—a national style.

Influences there undoubtedly were bearing on the form and on the style of decoration employed at Copenhagen. Luplau had little technique to learn. He came as a maturely trained modeller from Fürstenberg, which accounts for the fact that busts and statuettes were produced at a much earlier date in the history of the Copenhagen than in a factory having slowly to train its modellers. But undoubtedly a close examination of the porcelain of the Müller period exhibits the fact that there was a fine reticence applied to the form and the decoration which stands out in strong contrast to the extravagances and reckless prodigality of ornament employed by factories with older traditions. The new factory at Copenhagen was endowed with a sense of beauty from the first. The rococo style prevalent then at Meissen and dominating art is seldom found in old Danish porcelain; now and again its presence is noticeable and indicates that the work is of the early experimental days. But Copenhagen created a characteristic and natural style of its own, not only in the choice of Danish or Norwegian subjects, but in its intense love of nature and of simple forms.

The whole series of fine *pot-pourri* vases with natural flowers in relief is essentially different from Meissen examples where the vase is overloaded with fancifully modelled flowers and leaves. The graceful form and subdued decoration of Copenhagen stand out in effective contrast.

Moreover, the flowers themselves were evidently copied direct from nature, and are executed with such skill and refinement that they still stand as ideals of technical and artistic perfection.

In regard to the modelling of figures, especially those in costume, the reticence of Copenhagen is noticeable in comparison with the *outré* cavaliers and dames in crinolines of the Saxon and other factories. The subdued colouring and the simple charm of the Danish figures places them in a gallery of their own. Nor must this be mistaken for insipidity or weakness of design. Judged by the highest canons of art, the quality of such creations indicates complete control and mastery of technique, and art in due subjection.

The outburst of strong national intensity, love of nature, breadth of conception, and virility of execution lasted at the most for twenty years. The verse on a plate:—

Enhver sin Sæk til Möllen bærer
Hvor tungt den ham end og besværer:

which may be turned into English:—
Each man to the mill must bear his sack
Although the load may break his back—

was the leading precept of the staff under Müller. All worked together with single-heartedness of purpose, and the result is the admiration of all who love ceramic art, purposeful, and instinct with grace and dignity.

The Diversity of Designs.—The illustrations accompanying this chapter will show the range of subjects executed under the masterly *régime* of Müller. At first vases and services for royal use were made, but as soon as the retail establishment in 1780 enabled persons outside the royal *entourage* to purchase the porcelain, the feet of the factory were set on a rock. Similar forms to those embellished with royal ciphers and monograms and portraits were subsequently employed for persons of lesser degree.

The portrait of Müller shows him to have been a keen, virile, determined man, as we know, of endless resources, and possessed of abnormal energy. In less than twenty years there had been a constant and untiring enthusiasm in order to bring the factory to such perfection that it would be able to compete with the older and larger factories of Meissen, Berlin, and Sèvres. Perhaps this object was not achieved, inasmuch as the little factory did not enter into the lists to win European approval, but it succeeded in developing a national style, and this in spite of the fact that at the early stages it worked on foreign suggestion and employed foreign artists. Owing to the crowd of smaller factories at that date assimilating the technique and copying the designs of Meissen, it has come to be erroneously believed, owing to the looseness of generalization by writers on the subject and the absence of detailed study of Copenhagen porcelain of that period, that the Danish factory was another echo of Meissen or Berlin. The contemporary opinion of the two French counts, men of practised skill in observation and keen critics in regard to comparing the state of technique and conditions of manufacture of one country with another, comes as a complete refutation to the belief that Copenhagen was then in the second rank.

In regard to Müller's technical achievements, they stand to this day as a permanent record of his mastery of his art. The new body which he invented and called "virgin paste" is of a clear dazzling white, and is covered with a glaze transparent and smooth as polished crystal, tinted with the green of the sea; this glaze enhanced the beauty of the porcelain. Considering the impure materials then available, and the primitive working methods (for instance, fuel used at that time was wood, in poles 10 feet long of pine and fir), the perfection and beauty of the results demand profound admiration. Even with the aid of modern technology and chemistry it has not yet been found possible at the factory to produce porcelain equal in every respect to the old Müller period.

PASTILLE BURNER AND COVER.

On tripod stand with modelled dolphins as supports. Moulded cherub heads, and gilded banded wreath in high relief. Perforated cover surmounted by gilded pine-cone ornament.

The diverse character of the output was stupendous. It was rich in design, varied and original in invention, virile in modelling, and national in spirit. The beautiful body invented by Müller had its decoration with his perfected overglaze colours, green and blue and purple. In regard to gilding, the artistic ideal seems to have been attained. It is not possible to convey as illustrations in this volume the extraordinary variety and beauty exhibited in this field. In the cups and saucers herein illustrated, the fine quality of the designs is lost in translation, but these borders of deep blue enriched with gilded designs of the most exquisite character are something to marvel at in connection with the work of the Müller period.

The creations of the factory cover a wide range. The versatility of the modellers and the artists is pronouncedly marked. It bespeaks a great and prolific period when ideas were not lacking. Evidently there was no great searching after novelty, the gold was not beaten thin, apparently there was a profusion of intellectual force behind the factory. The difference is noticeable as soon as the great period is passed, when one falls on barren ways and thinly eked out inventions, the long years of the dreary twilight.

The love of landscape especially appealed to Copenhagen. The colours of the ceramic artist have limitations peculiarly their own. Atmosphere is rare in overglaze painting. There is a tendency to prettiness and an absence of breadth. But with pigments so refractory there are instances of work surprisingly powerful. Single colour scenes fare best, and there is one example in purple, poor enough medium, which has qualities almost suggesting the strength of a Dutch etching, as shown on a cup and saucer in the *Dansk Folke Museum*. The picturesque in colour finds its exposition in two octagonal dishes with sporting subjects. The one shows a man with a hound (illustrated, p. 93), and the other a man with a red coat engaged in the pastime of hawking.

Vases with portraits secured their patrons. There is one at the *Kunstindustri Museum* at Bergen; with the portrait of G. W. Rabener, born at Leipsic in 1714 and died in 1771, the friend of Klopstock, and the good-humoured satirist of German *bourgeois* society.

OCTAGONAL DISH.
With figure subject, Huntsman with hound, finely painted in colours. Blue border with rich gold decoration.

Apart from colour and decoration, there is the fine modelling. The symmetry of the more important vases, instinct with decorative qualities of the highest order, having ornament in relief, moulded garlands, gay Cupids, or mask handles of some wood-god, is always paramount. Rarely is there a false note.

To form and the mastery of the difficulties and the due observance of the technique of the potter, it is necessary to devote another chapter in which the illustrations convey sufficient evidence to show that projecting limbs and fantastic shapes more suitable to the metal-worker were eschewed at Copenhagen. The essentials of ceramics were never lost sight of by the band of modellers working under Müller.

National Sentiment.—There is a vein of sentiment, very pleasing and very piquant, running through much of the work of this period. It is the under-note of the potter, who, as other potters of other nations have before him, desired to convey a written message as well as the message in line, in colour, and in beauty of form that he set before his generation. Centuries before Müller, the Chinese potter revelled in his inscriptions. Potters the world over apparently are poets. On an old Chinese porcelain vase painted in blue, with a garden scene by moonlight, the following inscription in Chinese is found:—

"Heaven and earth are the associates of creation, as light and darkness are the passing guests of a hundred generations. Fleeting life is like a dream; how long do we enjoy it? It was this knowledge that made men in the old days trim the midnight lamp. And now Yang Chun invites us with smoke to illuminate the world with literature, to associate the fragrant gardens of the peach and the plum, and to talk of happiness. All graciously join me, and as they chant and sing, I alone am ashamed; they become vivacious, I in solitude rejoice. With loud talk they grow merry; a scholar's feast is spread, and sitting amid the flowers we pass the goblet quickly and drink till we are drunken. When the moon is not in its splendour, how can one expatiate on its ecstasy? But if my verses are not perfect I am fined the customary gold and the embarrassing wine."

Here is the Chinese potter—almost Viking-like in his song of the wine-cup in place of the wassail-bowl. Or shall it be the Persian astronomer-poet Omar Khayyám with his—

The Grape that can with Logic absolute
The Two-and-seventy jarring Sects confute:
The subtle Alchemist that in a Trice
Life's leaden Metal into Gold transmute.

The Staffordshire potters to a man loved a rhymed couplet on a jug or mug or punch-bowl, and their crude efforts amuse the latter-day collector. Their subjects were varied in character—loyalty, naval victories, courtship, and conviviality, with a smack of religion, as, for instance:—

Drink to live and live to die
That you may live eternally.

TRAY.

With oval panel with landscape painted in deep green. Wreaths around panel in purple. Finely gilded at borders. Painted by Elias Meyer.

Given by Frederik VI to Pastor Mandal, Sörum, Norway, 1790.
(*At the Kunstindustri Museum, Copenhagen.*)

There are many pretty sentiments found on Müller's ware. We have already quoted one (p. 87), and there are many mottoes inscribed in Danish on the porcelain of his period. There is the long inscription on the cup with his portrait (see p. 69), and there are others which we have translated as follows:—

Art bends nature to herself that clay
By magic is transformed to gold alway;

31

and an inscription on another example, translated runs:—
Long live the King, and glorious be his reign;
Long live ourselves to drink this toast again.

In the collection at Rosenborg Castle there is a cup and saucer upon which the letter F is painted in forget-me-nots. It is dated November 22, 1797, with this inscription:—

Uforglemmelige ungdomsaar for mig!
(Years of youth, unforgettable for me!)

We wonder for whom this initial F stands. The permanently abiding sentiment enshrined behind the glass case is to-day as fresh as the forget-me-nots. What romance lies hidden in these four Danish words burnt into the clay? But the records are silent, and F the giver or the receiver is turned into dust, while the potter's clay stands to symbolize an old-world story of the days when youthful ambitions and dreams lit up the memory.

TABLE OF MARKS[5]

Found on Royal Copenhagen porcelain with decoration painted overglaze of the Frantz Heinrich Müller period (1775-1801).

[5] These marks are strictly copyright.

These signatures and initials of painters and modellers, either painted or incised, are found in conjunction with the usual factory mark of the three blue lines.

General

The usual Factory Mark, in blue, found alone or in addition to painter's or modeller's signature or initials.

This mark was adopted at the suggestion of Queen Juliane Marie in 1775, and symbolizes the three waterways of Denmark—the Sound, and the Great and Little Belts.

This mark has been used on all porcelain made at the Royal Copenhagen Factory, both with overglaze and underglaze painted decoration, since that date.

N.B.—From 1773-1775 the porcelain of the Copenhagen factory made by Müller bore no mark.

Signature of Anton Carl Luplau, who came to Copenhagen in 1776, and died in 1795.

A *Bust of Queen Juliane Marie* at Rosenborg Castle bears this signature on base:—

Luplau fec:
1781

Signature of Hans Clio, who was working at the factory prior to 1779, and who died in 1786.

H. Clio

Peter Heinrich Benjamin Lehmann. Came to the factory in 1780. Died 1808. Painter of landscapes, figures, and birds.

Lehman

Signature of Hans Christopher Ondrup (1779-1787). Sometimes signed *Ondrup mahlt (Ondrup painted it)*. Painted signature frequently in red.

This signature in full has been traced from an example in the collection of Count Chr. Danneskjold-Samsöe, at Gissenfeldt.

Ondrup

Ondrup mahlt

H: C: O:

Signature of Andreas Hald (1781-1797), modeller and sculptor. Frequently marked his pieces in full or with initials **AH** incised. In some instances his initials are painted in blue on side of base, as in Figure of Flute Player (illustrated, p. 127).

A. Hald

A.H.

A H

Jesper Johansen Holm. Born 1747. Member of Royal Academy. Incised mark, **HOLM 1780** on *Statuette* at *National Museum*, Stockholm. (See illustration, p. 115.) **I HOLM 1781** incised marked on a *Bust of Prince Frederik* at *Kunstindustri Museum*, Copenhagen.

HOLM
1780

Signature of Johan Christoph Baÿer. Came to Copenhagen in 1768. Died 1812. Landscape painter, followed the style of Johann Christoph Dietsche, of Nuremberg (1710-1769). Engaged on painting the flowers in the *Flora Danica* service.

J . C . Baÿer

The mark of Jacob Schmidt, modeller and sculptor. He was, in 1779, a pupil at the factory in his fourteenth year. He died in 1807. Many of his pieces have his initials incised. An example at the *Dansk Folke Museum*, Copenhagen, has this mark together with the three lines *incised*, which is an exceedingly rare mark.

Incised mark on a cream cup and cover at the *Kunstindustri Museum*, Copenhagen, decorated with purple flowers and rococo ornamentation, gilded, and having scale-pattern in red. This mark (signifying that the piece belongs to the Christian VII era) is unusual. This may be conjectured to be a specimen made by Müller prior to 1775, that is, before the adoption of the mark of the three blue lines.

The incised mark of Hans Meehl, who was a modeller at the factory in 1791. This mark is found on a polychrome *Figure of a Man* in national costume (*Norsk Bjergmund*), at the *Kunstindustri Museum*, Copenhagen.

This mark is incised on the base of a polychrome figure of a *Woman with Hens* at the *Kunstindustri Museum*, Copenhagen.

LIST OF LEADING PAINTERS AND MODELLERS[6]

Who worked at the Royal factory under the Direction of Frantz Heinrich Müller (1773-1801).

[6] For the leading facts contained herein, I am indebted to Professor Karl Madsen in his article in *Tidsskrift for Kunstindustri*, 1893.

Anton Carl Luplau. 1776-1795.

Was at the Fürstenberg factory for eighteen years. Müller visited Luplau at Brunswick in 1776, and on November 14th an agreement was signed, and Luplau joined the Copenhagen factory as modelling-master. He died in 1795. He was a perfect craftsman. Many of his pieces were signed, e.g. the Bust of Queen Juliane Marie. Luplau made many of the models for the *Flora Danica* service, and executed 20 Norwegian types after the well-known sandstone figures at Fredensborg.

Claus Tvede. 1775-1783.

Sculptor and modeller at the factory. He is supposed to have made the Statuette of the Hereditary Prince Frederik after the design by Ludovico Grossi, which piece bears the initials of the modeller Andreas Hald.

Johan Christoph Baÿer. 1776-1812.

Born in Nuremberg 1738. Came to Denmark in 1768. Agreement signed on November 16, 1776, when he entered the service of the factory. He died in his seventy-fifth year, in 1812. Landscape painter; followed the style of Johann Christoph Dietsche, Nuremberg landscape painter (1710-1769). Executed drawings for Holmskjold's book on *Danish Fungi*. Entrusted with the work of flower painting on the *Flora Danica* service.

Hans Clio. Working before 1779. Died in 1786.

Painter. Appointed drawing-master to train the pupils at the factory. His signature appears on some of the porcelain with landscapes painted by him.

Lars Hansen. 1777-1800.

Born in 1739. In 1777 he is noted as being one of the best painters in blue underglaze ware. He died in 1800.

Jacob Schmidt. 1779-1807.

Born in 1764. Modeller and sculptor. At factory in 1779 as pupil in modelling in his fourteenth year. Many of his pieces are marked with his initials incised.

Hans Christoph Ondrup. 1779-1787.

Painter. His signature, or his initials, painted in red, is found on several pieces.

Peter Heinrich Benjamin Lehmann. 1780-1808.

Born in 1752 at Hamburg. Came to the factory from Berlin in 1780. Was naturalized in 1781 and died in 1808. He was a painter of landscapes, figures, and birds.

G. Kalleberg. 1780-1810.

Modeller of figures and *repoussé* worker. He appears to have had a large share in the production of figures and moulds, and there is presumptive evidence that his work was of a superlative character.

Jesper Johansen Holm. 1780-1802.

Modeller. Born in 1747. Member of the Royal Academy. Trained by Wiedevelt, the sculptor. His statuettes are finely executed. See *A Hero* (with **I HOLM 1780** incised mark), illustrated, p. 115, at National Museum, Stockholm. He became model-master in 1802.

Abildgaard. 1780-

Danish artist and sculptor, returned to Copenhagen from Continental travels in 1777, and brought new impulses. Consulted as adviser to factory in regard to art matters and correctness of modelling.

Martin Cadewitz. 1780-1791.

Served eleven years at factory. Died in 1791.

Johan Camrath, *Senior*. 1780-1796.

Portrait painter. Executed work for the factory till 1796. Died in 1814, in his seventy-sixth year. He was engaged on fine vases, and painted grey medallion panel portraits of Queen Juliane Marie, and other royalties, for important pieces. There is a small cup at Rosenborg Castle with the portrait of P. A. Heiberg painted by him. He was not permanently at the factory, but undertook work of a highly artistic nature.

Nicolaj Christian Faxoe. 1783-1810.

Born in 1762. Pupil at the factory in painting, 1783. Flower painter. Worked at the factory till his death in 1810.

Sören Preus. 1784-

Modeller. Executed the delicate flowers in relief on vases, baskets, and groups. The vases with Cupids and garlands, and the magnificent vase, with portrait of Queen Juliane Marie painted by Camrath, having a Cupid seated on body of vase amidst a garland of exquisitely moulded flowers and two lions finely modelled on cover, is the work of Sören Preus.

The baskets of flowers and bouquets and ornaments in the dessert centre pieces of the *Flora Danica* service suggest his master-hand.

Elias Meyer. 1785-1809.

Born in 1763 at Copenhagen, trained at Dresden. Flower and landscape painter. He occasionally marked pieces with his name. His work is not in the first flight. He died in 1809 as member of the Royal Academy.

M. Meyer. 1784-1792.

This artist was mentioned in conjunction with Camrath by Count Louis de Boisgelin, who visited the factory thirteen years after it had been founded. M. Meyer "is much esteemed for the beauty of his designs." It appears that both he and Camrath were not actually in the factory service on a fixed salary, but received payment for each piece executed.

Andreas Hald. 1781-1797.

Modeller and sculptor. This artist modelled a number of gracefully conceived figures. He frequently signed his work either A. Hald or with initials, incised, sometimes initials painted in blue, as on figure of *Flute Player*. See illustration, p. 127.

Johan Arentz. 1786-1796.

N. Bau. 1791-1820.

Landscape painter, animals and figures, *genre* subjects of peasants, and also silhouettes. Bau was the head painter from 1812. He died in 1820.

Many of his landscape subjects are painted in purple.

Johannes Ludvig Camrath, *Junior*. 1794-

Flower and fruit painter. Born in 1779. Became pupil at factory in 1794. Died in

1849.

Carl Fridrich Thomaschefsky. 1780-

This painter, originally trained at Berlin, worked only a short time at the factory. A colleague of Lehmann.

Raben Svardahlyn. Hans Jacob Hansen. Christian Ahrensborg. Matthias Wolstrup. Schaltz.

These painters were engaged on the underglaze mussel-blue painted ware during the Müller *régime*, together with Lars Hansen, who, in 1777, was considered the leading painter in this style.

CHAPTER IV

FIGURE SUBJECTS
AND GROUPS
(1780-1820)

CHAPTER IV

FIGURE SUBJECTS AND GROUPS
(1780-1820)

The inauguration of new impulses, 1780—Luplau, the modelling-master—The figure subjects of Kalleberg—Classification of figure subjects—Old Copenhagen figures, their national character—The last days of Müller.

Apart from the royal busts and statuettes, the sumptuous vases with portraits of royalties, and the magnificent services made for royal use or for some important personage, culminating in the great and extensive *Flora Danica* service, there were other examples, notably figure subjects and groups, often of a minor character, and vases and services of less splendour in their decoration but not of inferior character.

The date of these may be determined as subsequent to the year 1780, when a retail establishment was opened in Copenhagen in the heyday of Müller's triumph, for the sale of the factory productions. An outburst of popular feeling hailed this adventure with delight. The chronicles of the time are full of the subject. Hitherto great and important pieces were made under the Court patronage of Queen Juliane Marie and of Prince Frederik, her son, and important subjects were executed, giving to this period a character and dignity not surpassed by many of the older factories. But the royal factory now became the national factory. Henceforth merchants, burghers, the professional classes, and the Danish public in general were enabled to see a permanent exhibition of the ware of the Royal Porcelain Factory, and to purchase or give orders for a national ware which, naturally, was supplanting the use of all others in the country. In the year 1790 the importation of any foreign porcelain save Chinese was prohibited by law.

From 1780 to 1790 one may expect to find the factory in full enjoyment of success, particularly in regard to its manufacture and sale of utilitarian blue fluted services, underglaze painted, and of small figures and vases, overglaze painted, of a less magnificent character, designed for use and ornament in the home rather than representative of types more fitted for presents to foreign princes and plenipotentiaries. In 1790 Müller was fifty-eight years of age. In 1801 he had retired from the factory.

This chapter, while including important figures and groups, deals with types of a class which may be termed as in the second flight of Müller's artistic triumphs, and be it said much of the work is contemporary with more ambitious creations equal in character to some of the finest.

STATUETTE ENTITLED *A HERO.*
With incised Mark HOLM/1780 and three blue lines painted.
Height 12-1/5 inches.
(*At the National Museum, Stockholm.*)

As many of these minor pieces are dated and others have the signature of the artist or modeller, it is possible to arrive, with some degree of accuracy, at the period of their manufacture. Contemporary with all these overglaze painted examples of the factory one must not lose sight of the fact that the mussel-blue underglaze painted ware was continuously being made. New forms were being added, and its decoration with the "Danish pattern" adhered closely to the original floral *motif* now perennial to the ware.

Luplau, the Modelling Master.—In regarding the figure subjects, it must be borne in mind that the foreign assistance which Müller called in at the inception of the factory had not a little influence on the early and sure production of figures which could not have been attempted without experienced supervision. Under Anton Carl Luplau, the modelling-master who came to Copenhagen from the Fürstenberg factory, where he had spent eighteen years, the early stages of the Copenhagen modelling show a completer mastery of the technique than is usually exhibited by so young a factory.

But design and modelling, excellent though they undoubtedly were in the hands of Luplau, were only factors in the problem towards perfected results. The body, the glaze, and the colours were Müller's. Nor is it to be supposed that Luplau contributed more than the idea, practical without doubt, but it is improbable that he carried his supervision beyond the plastic stages. All credit is due to him for instilling the principles of fine lines and graceful forms into the minds of the young potters. But it was Müller by day and by night, with long vigils, often all night, at the ovens with his workmen whom he was training to control the caprice of the furnace, who seized the situation and gladly profited by experience in his uphill struggle to establish his factory in the face of all difficulties. Müller had the genius of "moulding men in plastic circumstance." Nor was Luplau the swan he is sometimes thought to have been. There is a suggestion in one of Müller's letters to the board of management of the factory which illuminates the inner history. Speaking of Luplau, and probably the old story—the cost of production—he says: "On the contrary, he demands extra payment for any work which he does himself, and as the factory cannot afford this, most of the figures and moulds are made by Kalleberg, and in this work Luplau appears to take a very small share."

TWO FIGURES OF SEA HORSES.

Painted in colours, brown predominating on a white ground. Each marked with three blue lines. Height 3-3/4 inches. Length 6-3/10 inches.

(*In the National Museum, Stockholm.*)

The Figure Subjects of Kalleberg.—The fertility of the early Copenhagen period when masterpieces, full of charm and perfect in style, rapidly appeared one after another in a short but crowded period, has puzzled students of the old period. To accept Luplau as the creator of them all, is to believe him classic and precise, and at the same moment capable of transforming his style into elegant, restrained creations of gaiety and fanciful forms in due subjection. To omit the subtle and critical examination of style is to fall into the pit which contains those curious mortals who believe the exact, terse, and laboured prose of Bacon to be by the author of *A Midsummer Night's Dream* and *Hamlet*. To such, it is possible to credit Julius Cæsar with having written the ode of Horatius Flaccus to *Lyde*.

There is some mystery as to the designer of the dancing figures, the flute-player, the lady at the tea-table, the Copenhagen group, the Norwegian dalemen in Fredensborg, the mountain-men, and certain dainty Cupids. They differ entirely from Laplau's productions in every respect, and stand far above them in artistic merit. The late Professor Krohn, whose patient researches, on this and other vexed questions concerning old Copenhagen porcelain, were unfortunately broken off by his untimely death, was of the opinion that these figure subjects were the work of the *repoussé* worker Kalleberg. Authentic confirmation is lacking, other than the letter above quoted. Until further evidence is forthcoming and further investigations are made into the Müller period, we must accept the authentic pronouncement by Müller as the last word on the subject.

In regard to the employment of foreigners, it is certain that the experiment was not a success. Five workmen were inveigled from Meissen in 1776. Out of the five, probably induced by monetary considerations to quit the Meissen factory, two did not make an appearance in Copenhagen. Of the three who came, it seems that only one showed any great talent. It would appear, too, that they exhibited an arrogance that stirred up strife in the factory. They received higher wages than the Danish workmen and began to assume correspondingly superior manners, with the belief that the factory could not proceed without them. But Müller speedily put an end to this state of affairs by closing the factory gates against them, and when they attempted to break in, he had them turned out by force. With these experiences in mind, it is not surprising that when, at a later date, some English workmen from the Wedgwood factory desired employment, they received scanty consideration.

FIGURE GROUP (ONE OF A PAIR).
Painted in overglaze colours. Period 1780-1790. Marked with three blue

Classification of Figure Subjects.—The figure subjects under examination in this chapter may be divided into the following groups:—

Portrait Busts and Statuettes and Classic figures, in biscuit—

such as those of Queen Juliane Marie and the Hereditary Prince Frederik, and the statuette of *A Hero* at the National Museum, Stockholm (illustrated, p. 115)

Ornamental subjects, in white—

such as the centre-piece with the supporting Cupids at the *Dansk Folke Museum*, Copenhagen, and the remarkably fine vases, 4 feet high, at Frederiksborg, having powerfully modelled groups of female classic figures.

Classic figures and subjects, decorated in colours, overglaze—

such as the group *Flora and Minerva* by Jacob Schmidt and *Sea Horses* at the National Museum, Stockholm (illustrated, p. 119).

Romantic subjects in costume, decorated in colours, overglaze—

such as *Lovers with Cupid and Garlands* (illustrated, p. 123), and small figures of women and children in fanciful costume.

There is at Frederiksborg Castle a group—*Chinese Woman and Chinaman*, who is offering her a basket of fruit. This Oriental subject is very rare. Marked with three lines underglaze in blue, but the yellow overglaze pigment on base has turned the blue into three *green* lines.

Figure subjects in correct contemporary costume—practically a ceramic gallery faithfully reflecting the social character of the period—

such as the *Flute Player*, the *Lady and Gentleman dancing*, the *Beggar*, and an especially fine series of peasant types in old costume, engaged at their various vocations —e.g. two groups of *Norwegian Miners*, with black costume and green caps, with C7 in gold (at Frederiksborg Castle). The *Woman with Hens*, in Norwegian costume, a *Market Woman with Fowls*, a *Lobster-seller*, *Woman selling Fruit*, *Woman milking Cow*. Figures in naval and military uniform, and many others.

Old Copenhagen Figures—their National Character.—In regard to the series of figures in contemporary costume, there is an air about them which stamps them at once as being the work of the old Copenhagen factory. They are practically portrait studies, with that added touch of poetic charm which fits them for their place among the gods of the china cabinet.

They challenge comparison with the work of other European factories. Kändler, the modeller at Meissen, in what is styled the *Krinolinengruppen* period in mid eighteenth-century days, produced figures of lovers and ladies in rich costumes. They belong to that impossible world of the china-shelf, of shepherds and shepherdesses and bending cavaliers and gay ladies, conjured up in the fertile brain of the potter. They invaded France and they conquered England in the glorious days of Derby and Chelsea. But with a few notable exceptions they did not penetrate to Copenhagen.

FIGURES.
Old woman supplicating alms.
Man playing flute.
Marks.—A.H. incised on base, and A.H. painted in blue at side of base.
Height 6-3/8 inches.
(***At the Dansk Folke Museum, Copenhagen.***)

The groups of *Lovers with Cupids* and chains of roses are two examples of this romantic movement which came into the world of ceramics, a reflex of the decorative art of fashionable Court painters, who invented a topsy-turvy world of make-believe.

The quiet strength and the subdued restraint of the old Copenhagen figures stand out in contrast to this outburst of fanciful exuberance. The note of fidelity is as apparent in the figures in costume of the Müller period as it is noticeable in regard to floral decorations and modelled foliage taken direct from nature. Nor does this betray a want of imagination or a lack of ideality in choice of figure subjects. If it be classic, there is poetry in the statuette of *A Hero*, or a loose rein is given by the modeller to his *Sea Horses*, a poet's vision of the sea rollers leaping shore-wards from the Baltic. The fashion for the romantic did eventually tinge the Copenhagen *atelier*. Some of the little figures are graceful, retiring, modest examples of the movement. It is true they are decked in impossible costumes, but the mode has in the transplantation acquired simplicity and reticence. Some of them suggest, in porcelain, the quaint charm of Kate Greenaway's world of picturesque children.

Of the gallery of contemporary life the Copenhagen figures, in the main, are faithful likenesses. The dancing cavalier and lady (see *Frontispiece*) represent persons who actually did dance as they are modelled. There is nothing added except that touch of the modeller's genius in catching the rhythmical pose of the poetry of motion which crystallizes them as a work of art. The *Flute Player* is equally caught in the act, natural and unobtrusive. There is nothing affected in his attitude or in his costume (illustrated, p. 127). It is such traits as these which endear the old Copenhagen figures to connoisseurs. The glaze is rich and liquid and the colours are subdued in tone and appeal to lovers of subtlety in art. Whatever extraneous influences in art press upon the work of the Danish

potters, there is a process of refining which they seemingly undergo, and in so doing
     Suffer a sea change
 Into something rich and strange.

     As may be imagined, these old-world figures are much treasured by Danish collectors, who realize that they represent a national phase of art and form a record of quaint and forgotten costume. The sellers in the market-place, the women with fowls, the fisherman with the striped jersey and shiny hat familiar in old prints of our own sailormen, and the Admiral with his speaking trumpet—it might be the great Fischer himself, of the days when fleets were sweeping the North Sea and the Baltic—come with peculiar associations from bygone days.

FIGURE GROUPS.
Market woman with Fruit and Lobster seller. Height 6-2/5 inches.

FIGURES IN CONTEMPORARY NAVAL AND MILITARY UNIFORMS.
     Decorated in colour.
     (*From the collection of His Excellency the late M. de Bille.*)

The Last Days of Müller.—The illustrations herein given cover this diverse field and serve to indicate the versatility of the modellers who worked during the Müller period. The peasant types and some of the smaller figures belong to the latter days of the Müller *régime*. Although Müller retired from the factory in 1801, he kept in touch with what was in progress. His hand may not have been on the helm, but he had spirit enough left in his retirement to burst forth with pungent criticisms upon the later methods pursued, and there is no doubt the old veteran was frequently consulted by those upon whom his mantle had fallen. The fiery spirit of Müller, proof against all adversity, with the eye of the eagle saw across a longer space than men of ordinary vision. "Everything which has been done after I left the factory," growls out the fiery old man, "has been to its detriment." And who shall say that his words were not true?

Müller had heard the guns booming in the Sound in 1801, he had seen the havoc of bombardment by an alien fleet in 1807. His heart's desire, his beloved factory, had been wrecked. A great man's treasure-house of dreams had been devastated. The story of the ruin which overtook the factory comes with stunning poignancy with the knowledge that owing to the misery which followed the war the factory actually closed down in 1810, for a time, owing to the want of fuel. Years after the death of Müller and the glories of his day had departed, a number of his oldest models and moulds were found in a heap of shards stowed away in a loft in the old factory. At the removal to the new factory at Frederiksberg it was hardly thought worth while to carry them away.

Fortunately, this was done, and in spite of their wrecked condition, loving hands have pieced them together. It is now happily possible to reproduce faithfully some two hundred of the beautiful models of the great days.

Frantz Heinrich Müller, the greatest potter of Denmark, is not dead, although his ashes have lain in a nameless grave for nearly a century. His memory still lies green in the hearts of those who love great things finely conceived, great triumphs nobly won, and great dreams perfectly consummated.

CHAPTER V

THE *FLORA DANICA* SERVICE
(1790-1802)

MADE FOR CATHERINE II,
EMPRESS OF RUSSIA

CHAPTER V

THE *FLORA DANICA* SERVICE
(1790-1802)

MADE FOR CATHERINE II, EMPRESS OF RUSSIA

The Crown Prince Frederik (afterwards Frederik VI) orders the Flora Danica service to be made—A period of twelve years occupied in making it—The taste of the Empress Catherine II of Russia—Theodor Holmskjold, the botanist—The service.

A separate chapter is devoted to the great service executed by the Royal Copenhagen Factory during the years 1790 to 1802. It takes a place with other great services, the masterpieces of old and distinguished factories, such as the magnificent table service of *pâte tendre* Sèvres porcelain finished in 1778 for the Empress Catherine II of Russia, consisting of about 750 pieces and costing some £13,200. The Empress, it is interesting to read, considered this price exorbitant, and a lengthy diplomatic correspondence ensued. This service was part of the imperial collection at St. Petersburg. The celebrated Wedgwood dinner service of earthenware made for Catherine II and delivered in 1774, consists of painted English scenery, depicting famous views and noblemen's seats. This comprised over 950 pieces, and a portion of it was exhibited in London in 1909 by Messrs. Josiah Wedgwood and Sons, of Etruria, by permission of late His Imperial Majesty the Emperor of Russia.[7]

[7] See illustrated descriptive Catalogue of Wedgwood Exhibition, 1909, 4to, 22 pp., by the present writer, also *Connoisseur*, December 1909.

The *Flora Danica* service had as a patron the Crown Prince Frederik, the son of Christian VII and Queen Caroline Matilda. In 1784 another palace revolution had happened. The power of Queen Juliane Marie and her son, the king's brother, was broken. Prince Frederik (afterwards Frederik VI on the death of his father Christian VII, at the age of fifty-nine, in 1808) assumed the presidency of the State Council, after an unseemly struggle for the person of the imbecile king had taken place between him and his uncle Frederik, Prince Hereditary, resulting in the complete rout of the latter. The same day, April 14, 1784, the Crown Prince Frederik was proclaimed Regent. From that moment the rule of the Queen Dowager and her son Frederik was ended. She and her son retained their apartments at Christiansborg Palace, and Fredensborg was set apart for the use of Queen Juliane Marie. She lived in retirement until her death in 1796. Her son Frederik refrained from meddling in State affairs, and confined his attention to the welfare of art and science.

Frederik VI, endeared to his people more than any other Danish king, in spite of his military brusqueness, was as simple and frugal as our own Farmer-King, George III, whose grandson he was. Frederik's blue cotton umbrella is still exhibited as a relic in his apartments in Rosenborg Castle, and at his death, in 1830, all classes mourned the loss of a friend. Peasants bore the coffin of the old monarch tenderly to his last resting-place at Roskilde.

He was twenty years of age when Count Marshal Bülow, with a fatherly regard for the Crown Prince, and desirous of giving that touch of refinement denied the youth by the naturalistic theories of Struensee and the sterner methods of the Queen Dowager, took him from his military duties to pay early morning visits to the Royal factory. These glimpses into a world of artistry cannot have been other than stimulating to the young prince. Struensee's Rousseau-like training had made him a child of nature, and Juliane Marie had twisted him into the cast-iron grooves of a stiff and formal Court etiquette. In regard to art, he came at a time when the love of nature was becoming paramount. The age was rapidly shaking off the artificial. Sated with rococo ornament and with insipid and frivolous unrealities, the pendulum swung to the natural and to the essentially simple. Straight or shapely curved lines became the fashion. The period of *Louis Seize* had succeeded the rococo taste of *Louis Quinze* in Continental art.

The Taste of the Empress Catherine of Russia.—From 1784, when he made his *coup d'état*, Frederik advisedly gave important orders to the royal factory. In 1790 the *Flora Danica* service was ordered by the Crown Prince. It was not at first known for whom it was intended. The old factory books record it as "*Perle model broge malet med Flora Danica*" (Pearl body, colour painted with *Flora Danica*). As the service progressed it transpired that it was to be presented to Catherine II, Empress of Russia. The modern spirit was in the air, the new style was realistic and tinged with a scientific *motif*; moreover, it was to be a gift to a bluestocking. The Empress Catherine essayed to make her Court the centre of letters and art. At great cost she purchased the library of Diderot, and invited him to come to St. Petersburg to be the custodian of his own collection. She corresponded with Voltaire and she talked philosophy with Grimm, who, in his celebrated *Correspondance Littéraire*, kept her informed of the latest plays and books appearing in Paris. She established a French theatre in St. Petersburg, and fined absentee courtiers fifty roubles and sent her guards to bring in those who had failed to attend. French visionaries looked to Russia as a land of promise. Voltaire never tired of proclaiming that the Mohammedans should be driven out of Europe. And the Empress Catherine was to be the chosen instrument. The philosopher of Ferney, with his pen dipped in honey, writes:—

"*Si vous étiez souveraine de Constantinople votre majesté établirait bien vite une belle académie grecque; on vous ferait une Catériniade; les Zeuxis et les Phidias couvriraient la terre de vos images; la chute de l'empire ottoman serait célébrée en grec; Athènes serait une de vos capitales; la langue grecque deviendrait la langue universelle; tous les negocians de la mer Egée demanderaient des passeports de votre majesté.*"

The great Danish service was therefore to be a fitting present for so powerful a queen. For some twelve years the work was continued uninterruptedly. At first it was designed for eighty persons, and in 1794 no less than 1,835 pieces were ready. The death of the Empress Catherine II in 1796 precluded the service joining those of Sèvres and Wedgwood in the imperial palace at St. Petersburg. But its manufacture was still continued. In 1797 it had enlarged its dimensions, and was fit for a hundred persons. In 1802 it was stopped. If counted in English fashion, with lid, bowl, and stand as three pieces, the number had grown to three thousand pieces, or some two thousand, counting such vessels as one piece. The dessert service alone amounted to six hundred and twenty-three pieces, consisting of basket vases, flower and fruit stands, and, as is usual in dessert services, exceptionally fine examples, elegant, finely modelled, and exquisitely painted.

The date of the completion of the *Flora Danica* service practically coincides with the date of the retirement of Müller from the directorship of the factory, and therefore with this service ends the great and prolific Müller period.

In the examination of the *Flora Danica* service considerable attention has been paid to the artistic and decorative results, but insufficient study has been given to the causes which led to the inception of so scientific an idea in regard to the record of the national flora on a service of such importance.

FISH-DISH.
     With drainer having modelled trout painted in natural colours. From *Flora Danica* **service made for Catherine II, Empress of Russia.**
     (*At Rosenborg Castle, Copenhagen.*)

     Theodor Holmskjold, the Botanist.—The patron, as we have seen, was the Crown Prince Frederik. The artist entrusted with the painting of the work was A. C. Baÿer, but the guiding spirit of the enterprise undoubtedly was Theodor Holmskjold, who was a botanist of some distinction, had studied under the world-renowned Von Linné at Upsala, and was his favourite pupil. Holmskjold, a director of the factory throughout the great Juliane Marie period, and almost to the end of Müller's long control, brought the scientific spirit of exactitude into the field of decorative art. Originally by name Holm, he took, after his ennoblement in 1781, the title of Holmskjold. He was professor of medicine and natural history at Söroe, the Danish Eton, where he planned a botanical garden, and later he took part in the management of the Botanical Gardens at Copenhagen. His work on *Danish Fungi* is distinguished by the artistic excellence of the illustrations, which were made by Baÿer. In 1767 he became postmaster-general of Copenhagen. In 1772, the year of the masked ball at Christiansborg, we find him cabinet secretary to Queen Juliane Marie. Undoubtedly at that time the man of science put aside his dried specimens to join in the whirl of politics and Court intrigue which ended in the seizure of Struensee and Queen Matilda—the gallows-tree for the dictator and imprisonment for Denmark's young queen. The classification of *fungi* was seemingly little enough preparation for the pinking of Court butterflies, when plots of assassination were rife, and when the actors' heads were not secure on their shoulders. But Holmskjold, together with another student, Suhm, the historian, who came from his library and helped to make history, ably acquitted himself. He was a trusted confidant of Queen Juliane Marie. It was he who induced the queen to take up Müller's company, and himself (then Holm) became one of the directors.

Long after Queen Juliane Marie's power had waned, we find him true to his allegiance to her, as in 1792 he became chamberlain to her Court. His connection with Müller was intimate. A widower in 1780, Müller married Holm's somewhat elderly sister. In brother-in-law Holm Müller found a good patron. His position at the Court, his relationship with Müller, his intense desire to win renown for an enterprise to which he had himself obtained the royal appellation, made him at once a powerful and interested ally. He died in 1793, before the final completion of the great service to which his influence had contributed so much, but not before he had seen the establishment of the Royal Copenhagen porcelain under the *régime* of Queen Juliane Marie, his mistress, attain great eminence and distinction.

It is impossible to ignore Holmskjold's special and particular influence on the character of the decorations of the great Copenhagen Catherine II service. The personality of the botanist-director is here evident. But apart from this individual influence, in an examination of the causes likely to have contributed to the style of decoration employed, passing mention must be made of the great national enterprise planned by Oeder in 1761: the original idea being that all European Governments should contribute to a series of volumes illustrating the complete flora of Europe. By this scientific co-operation duplication was thus to be avoided, and each plant would be described once only.

Denmark alone took sufficient interest in the botanical work to complete it. Austria touched the fringe of her flora with five hundred illustrations, and Russia contributed a hundred. So the *Flora Danica*, under the guidance of several generations of botanists, ploughed its solitary furrow alone. The first volume, containing the first three parts, was issued by Oeder in 1766. The plants were painted *in situ* by zealous artist-botanists who travelled to the remote districts of Denmark. This magnificent undertaking was in its earliest stages when the great porcelain service was in contemplation.

It is interesting here to note the further history of the great botanical work. Five parts were issued by O. F. Müller from 1775 to 1787. Vahl, the great botanist, who died in 1804, followed on by another five parts, and the next seventeen parts, extending over a period of thirty-five years, were under the editorship of J. W. Horniman, who published a history of the progress of the work from its inception down to 1836. By royal decree in 1847 it was decided to accept illustrations of Swedish and Norwegian plants not found in Denmark, thus increasing the scope and value of the work. It was to be completed in fifty-one parts, and not until the year 1883 was this great botanical work of the *Flora Danica* pronounced finished!

It will thus be seen that, apart from Holmskjold's special and particular predilections, there were general and national impulses directed towards this work of exceptional character and of European importance. It may readily be imagined that, prior to the advent of the *Flora Danica* service, the artists at the royal factory who painted flowers had, under the vigilant eye of the specialist director, to paint them from nature. A convolvulus did not become so decoratively treated as to evade identification. The Greek honeysuckle pattern of conventional use would not have passed at Copenhagen. Conventionality was as much eschewed in decoration as was the rococo in modelling. It is thus evident that nature and nature study, so remarkable and beautiful a feature in Copenhagen porcelain, owes not a little to the trained scientific vision of Theodor Holmskjold, the botanist.

Other factors enter into the question of the consideration of this *Flora Danica* service. It is obvious that the national feeling in artistic and scientific circles was centred on nature and nature study. Jean-Jacques had shown mankind that Dame Nature was capable of being wooed with intense passion. It was not until the late eighteenth century that the beauties of landscape began to be assiduously sought after. Travellers crossed the Alps from one country to another and regarded the frowning mountain, the sombre pass, or the rushing torrent much in the same manner as the unpoetic mariner feared the hurricane. Nature in her majestic loneliness was appalling. The sunny slopes of the Apennines concealed volcanic terrors. The smile of the blue Lake of Como was as treacherous as the dancing waves of the fickle sea itself. Lakes and mountains and mountain gorges were to be avoided; no mortal had conceived the idea of discovering their beauty. They were as fearsome as the Pillars of Hercules to the Latin mariners.

CRUET STAND.
From *Flora Danica* service made for Catherine II of Russia.
(*At Rosenborg Castle, Copenhagen.*)

In England, Thomas Gray, the poet, made a journey into Westmoreland and Cumberland in 1765 to see the Lake Country. His letters are the first note in English literature of man's kinship with nature. It took a century for the modern thought to germinate—"great men are part of the infinite, brothers of the mountain and the sea." As early as 1739, Gray's letters to his mother are filled with passages extolling the grandeur of the crags and precipices of the Alps, at a time when Rousseau had not developed his later method, and Vernet had only commenced to paint the turbulent sea with ecstasy.

In Denmark, in 1790, when the first model of the *Flora Danica* service was turned on the potter's wheel, this inquiring and reflective spirit was in the air, and the general tendency manifestly found a reflex in the great national service being manufactured at the Royal Porcelain Factory. The Russian Government had already entered into co-operation in a small degree in regard to bringing the records of the Russian flora into line with that of Denmark, and Catherine II, as is known, was the patron of the German naturalist Dr. P. S. Pallas, who, in 1784, commenced a *Flora Russica*, which was to eclipse anything yet attempted. This was to be published at the expense of Catherine. At her wish Pallas had in 1768 undertaken a scientific expedition to Siberia, which occupied six years.

In this connection, therefore, and knowing the Empress Catherine to be a votary of science and of art, the services made in England, France, and Denmark for imperial use were not undertaken without due consideration of this fact. The Sèvres service was embellished with the art of the schools of Boucher, Lancret, and Watteau; the Wedgwood service was frankly topographical, having painted copies, in mulberry purple, of old engravings, and Copenhagen was designedly botanical, based on the coloured illustrations of the *Flora Danica* volumes.

The Service.—A notable visitor to the factory at the time of the inception of the *Flora Danica* service was the Chevalier Louis de Boisgelin, Knight of Malta, who published his *Travels through Denmark and Sweden* in English in two volumes, at London, in 1810. The Comte Alfonse de Fortia, his fellow-traveller, had previously published *Les Voyages de deux François dans le Nord de l'Europe*. As a trustworthy account of a contemporary eye-witness the opinion of de Boisgelin is quoted:—

"The most beautiful porcelain likely to be sent for a long time from this manufacture will be a complete service upon which is to be represented, in natural colours, all the plants of the *Flora Danica*, with one upon each piece, large or small, according to the dimensions of the piece. The name of the plant will be marked under the plate, and the whole is to be classed according to the Linnæan system. The drawings are traced with such wonderful accuracy, that the most famous painters belonging to the manufactory would not undertake so difficult and slavish a piece of work."

This last statement as to the mechanical accuracy required in the painting of the flora stamps it as something outside the realm of the ordinary flower painter, and indicates at once the extreme scientific definition of drawing required.

The Royal Copenhagen Factory had come to be recognized by other Continental factories as excelling in the modelling of flowers, and as exhibiting truthful and natural beauty in their employment for decorative effect. The originality of the shapes of this service in comparison with those of contemporary factories shows them to possess a fine reticence which does not detract from the grand and imposing character of the imperial service. The border is a new and bold treatment with serrated leaf design, richly gilded and having three rows of gilt pearls. In point of decoration the new style is realistic, but far too scientific in treatment.

As a service it is magnificent. It amply fulfils the great and inspired conceptions of its originators. Luplau was still a modeller, skilful and practised in his own field of dignified, restrained, and well-balanced forms compelling admiration, and the bouquets and floral ornaments were modelled by Sören Preus. In painted decoration the scientific atmosphere is only too evident. Baÿer's pencil too faithfully followed the botanical volumes of the *Flora Danica*. Each piece is different; the whole gamut of the flora was covered, but each subject was obviously not equally suitable for decorative effect. True decorative art, however realistic, is alien from scientific exactitude.

The plants with their roots, leaves, and cross-sections of the stems evade decorative treatment. The scientific spirit is further exhibited in the written Latin names and references to the text of *Flora Danica* appearing at the back of each piece. But it must be reiterated that it was intended as a present to a votary of Von Linné, and the scientific study of nature had challenged the capture of nature by art.

The magnificence of the great service is the magnificence of a great series of ceramic volumes, reflecting in another medium the triumphs of the illustrated volumes of the *Flora Danica*.

It is the first instance of the Copenhagen factory searching for designs in a domain foreign to the true natural sources of inspiration proper to the artist designer on porcelain. Another and later instance is the series of imitative porcelain statuettes after Thorvaldsen's creations in marble.

CHAPTER VI

EARLY BLUE-AND-WHITE
UNDERGLAZE PAINTED

CHAPTER VI

EARLY BLUE-AND-WHITE UNDERGLAZE PAINTED

The "Danish Pattern"—The Bornholm Clay period—Peculiarities in marking— Table of Marks (old blue-and-white underglaze painted porcelain).

The blue-and-white underglaze painted porcelain of Copenhagen has become recognized as characteristic of the royal factory and of Denmark. The original design is of Chinese origin, in common with other forms of decoration, centuries old, followed by all European potters in early days when the art of making true porcelain was discovered in the West. But, like many another transplantation in art, it found congenial atmosphere, and has become national to the country of its adoption. The light, graceful plant *motif* shown in the blue-and-white painted fluted porcelain is as welcome a sight to Danes the world over as the slender twin spires of Roskilde Cathedral, where the kings of Denmark sleep in eternal peace.

The "Danish pattern" bears in a measure a certain relationship to works in literature where the translation is greater than the original.

This is especially true when the work of a decadent period is translated into the richer tongue of a more golden age. The English Bible translated in the time of James I is richer in its fine wealth of prose than the "original sacred tongues."

Some arts have been lost. It is said that the art of translation has never been discovered. All have laboured after it in vain; it is as hard to seek as hidden treasure, and one never finds it. But the Royal Copenhagen Porcelain Factory found the "hidden treasure" in the design which has grown into a thousand shapes inspired by the traditions of Müller, who "laid the East in fee," and whose successors true to his memory are not those

Who would keep an ancient form
Through which the spirit breathes no more.

From the manor farms of Vendsyssel to the confines of Danish-built Altona, from the white cliffs of Möen to the ancient roofed city of Ribe, the blue-and-white underglaze painted porcelain plates and dishes have been family heirlooms since the days of Christian VII.

GROUP OF UNDERGLAZE, BLUE PAINTED.
Bornholm Period.
(*In Museum of Royal Porcelain Factory, Copenhagen.*)

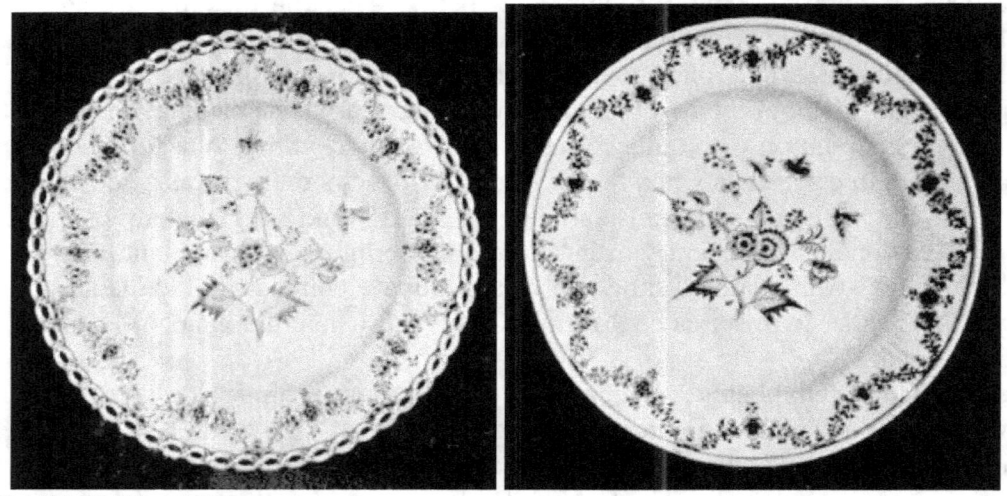

EARLY PLATES.
Painted in blue underglaze, showing variation of national Danish pattern.
(*At Dansk Folke Museum, Copenhagen.*)

The *Flora Danica* service represents the greatest complete creation in the overglaze painted work of the royal factory, and this blue-and-white stands as the greatest and most complete creation of the underglaze work.

It has been advanced, and on sure grounds, that this Copenhagen blue-and-white porcelain, with its continuity of national design extending in unbroken line for over a century and a quarter, is the largest service the world has seen. It has grown by steady process of evolution into thousands of well-defined forms, rich in inventive modelling, and keeping abreast with modern requirements, and it is to this day decorated with the old pattern of the early days. This of itself is an achievement not equalled by any other factory. A Copenhagen breakfast set of the twentieth century or a *tête-à-tête* tea service can stand beside eighteenth-century blue-and-white porcelain from the same factory, and be in perfect harmony in colour, in decoration, and in character.

Kindred and allied by birth,
And made of the same clay.

The "Danish pattern" in blue was not long in attracting copyists from other European factories. To-day in Copenhagen itself English faience transfer-printed in blue stands as a trade imitation and a tribute to the genius and originality of its prototype. Possibly the potter plagiarists may never have heard of the pregnant words of Goethe: "There are many echoes, but few voices."

The Bornholm Clay Period.—Mention has already been made, in dealing with the early discoveries of Müller and the experiments he made, of the clay which he found in the island of Bornholm. This clay forms the body of some of the earliest-known pieces made by him. It may be readily recognized by its heavy weight and by its grey tone. It is easy, after making an examination of a great number of specimens of the old blue-and-white ware, to distinguish this Bornholm period, even although in the two years (1773-1775) prior to the adoption of the three blue lines as a factory mark, some pieces bear no mark whatever. It somewhat resembles certain heavy Japanese ware in its compact and solid body and grey-blue colour.

The author has made a fairly exhaustive test of several hundred pieces, both in public and in private collections. The gradual development in regard to the perfection of the paste and the glaze is so noticeable that it is possible to place the old blue-and-white fluted ware in successive grades according to the stages of evolution. At first coarse, though never meaningless nor offensive, when the ware was obviously in an experimental period, it betrayed fire-cracks and warpings in form and slight departures from perfect symmetry. Later it became whiter and thinner, and was manifestly more completely under the control of the potter. When the perfected period was reached, there were tea caddies, pounce boxes, and, in particular, certain dishes, of which an example is illustrated (p. 169) which are not unworthy to be compared favourably with specimens of old blue-and-white Worcester of the early period. There is a delicacy and refinement in the modelling and potting, and that tenderness in the glaze and thinness in the body which at once betoken that the technique has been subjected to the patient potter's control.

GROUP, PAINTED IN BLUE UNDERGLAZE.
Tea Caddy, circular. Mark, three lines, figure 1 (blue); II (incised).
Teapot. Fine rich blue. Mark, three lines and figure 3 on lid.
Tea Caddy. Mark, three lines, figure 2 and two lines (blue); T (incised).
(*In Museum at Royal Copenhagen Porcelain Factory.*)

DISH (NATIONAL DANISH PATTERN), AND TWO PLATES.
Decorated with underglaze blue painting.

Peculiarities in Marking.—For the first time in any treatment of the subject, the potters and modellers' marks are given in a table appended to this chapter, which the writer hopes will be found useful in identifying early examples. These hieroglyphics, usually accompanied by the factory mark of the three blue lines, are painters' marks, and in the case of incised marks are representative of the modellers or turners. It may be possible, upon further research being given to the subject, to identify the individual marks of each painter or modeller, and thus arrive at some more definite conclusion in regard to the date at which these early blue-and-white pieces were made. But until the exact list of painters at the factory, together with the dates at which they were employed, is subjected to exhaustive research, it is obviously impossible to establish more than the present series of marks, with limited conclusions in regard to chronological order. The marks now given have been specially drawn from old examples of undoubted authenticity.

There is one peculiarity in connection with the marks found on this early blue-and-white porcelain. The bases are frequently ground, and the factory mark of the three blue lines, with an accompanying painter's mark, are on the base, with little spots of glaze put over them no bigger than a threepenny-piece. Another idiosyncrasy of Copenhagen marks, not confined to the blue-and-white, is the almost hidden position in which some of the marks are found. In overglaze painted figures the three blue lines will peep from beneath the hem of some garment. In the blue-and-white examples the mark is sometimes found on the inside of the handle of a teapot or on a lid. In some of the earlier pieces the blue mark has turned to black under the action of the oven. Similarly, in the early days of experiments in connection with the perfecting of the blue, a series of plates will be found of exactly the same decoration and bearing the same painter's signature; but the caprice of the fire, or the inexact knowledge of the craftsman, has converted the blue of some of them into a very deep blue, approaching black in tone.

There is no doubt that the old blue-and-white porcelain of Copenhagen has not yet been exploited by collectors. It came concurrently with the rich overglaze painting in colours and the magnificence of gilding for which the Müller period is remarkable. It stands quite apart; its decoration is underglaze, and not at that time, nor since, has gold ever been added to this mussel-blue painted and fluted utilitarian ware other than in very exceptional circumstances. It is simple and delightful, and what it was in the old days it is now. The style of painted decoration is perennial. It is a pattern known all over the world. It has lived for a hundred and thirty-six years. Its life-history suggests the long-continued idealities of the Chinese potter or the coloured intricacies of the Persian rug-weaver continued by the wise children of clever craftsmen with equal fidelity from generation to generation.

TABLE OF MARKS

(Old Blue-and-white Porcelain Underglaze Painted)

of Painters and Modellers, found usually in conjunction with the Factory Mark of the three blue lines. Painter's mark in blue. Modeller's mark incised.

Mark found on examples of the Bornholm clay period, see *Apothecary Jar* (illustrated, p. 161).

On *Oval Dish*, fine body, and with scale pattern decoration in rich blue. **MII** (incised). (Illustrated, p. 169).

Coffee Pot, Bornholm period, **ML** incised. (Illustrated, p. 161).

On a *Soup Tureen*, marked at bottom of vessel inside.

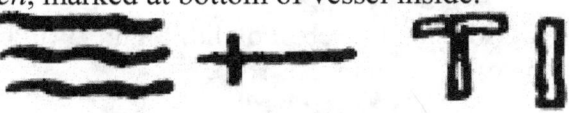

On a *Soup Tureen*, at bottom of vessel inside, **TI** on base (incised).

Bornholm period mark. On a *Pounce Box*, *Cup* with spout and handle, and other examples.

On a *Plate* with pierced edge (illustrated, p. 169).

On a round *Inkstand* Three lines and cross (in black). **K** (incised).

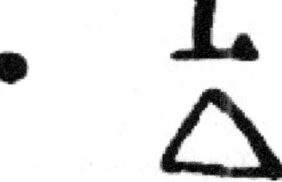

On a *Pounce Box*, at Museum, Royal Copenhagen Manufactory. **L** (incised).

On a round *Tea Caddy*, with floral decoration. **II** (incised).

On a *Tea Caddy*. Inside rim (in blue). **T** on base (incised).

On a *Small Teapot*. Moulded rosebud on lid. Figure 3 (in blue) on rim of lid. Other mark on base (in blue). (Illustrated, p. 167).

On a *Compotier* (in blue). At the Museum, Royal Copenhagen Porcelain Factory.

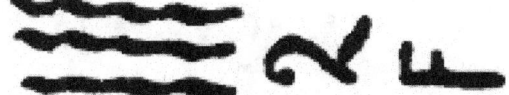

Mark (in blue) on *Plate* with pierced edge.

On a *Soup Tureen and Cover*, with lemon and leaves modelled on cover, natural size. Figure 2 (incised).

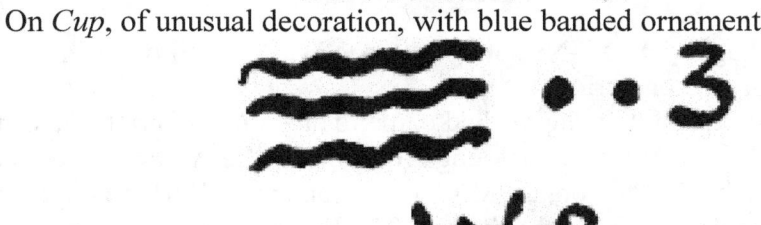

On a *Cup*, and other examples.

On a *Plate*, at Museum, Royal Copenhagen Factory, and other examples.

On *Cup*, of unusual decoration, with blue banded ornament.

On a *Fruit Basket*, pierced work, twisted handles, and roses in relief. **W2** (incised).

On a *Jug* at the *Dansk Folke Museum*, Copenhagen.

On a *Dish* at the *Dansk Folke Museum*, Copenhagen. Other numerals are found from 1 to 7.

CHAPTER VII

THE SUCCESSORS OF MÜLLER
(1820-1880)

THE DECADENCE

Battle of Copenhagen, 1801—Nelson's Letters to Lady Hamilton—The so-called Empire style—The Thorvaldsen period.

The great days of the Müller *régime* had come to an end. A quarter of a century of brilliant success was followed by twice that length of gloom. The Arctic night of early nineteenth-century years had settled on art. Müller's retirement in 1801 was not the only contributory cause of the decadence of the factory. The French Revolution had shaken Europe from end to end. The Napoleonic Wars following in its wake disturbed serenity and repose in art and letters. The fortunes of States were in the melting-pot, and destiny was "moulding men in plastic circumstance." The storm cyclone had more than once centred around Denmark. The century opened ill for the fortunes of the factory. In April 1801 a British fleet entered the Sound and engaged in a great naval battle with the Danish fleet. "I have been in a hundred and five engagements," said Nelson, "but that of to-day is the most terrible of them all." The genius of Napoleon conceived the idea of "conquering the sea by the land," to quote his own words. Paul I of Russia became Napoleon's ally and tool. Russia brought pressure to bear on Sweden, Denmark, and Prussia, and these Powers were federated as the "League of Armed Neutrality," with the avowed purpose of challenging the maritime supremacy of England. Prussia marched troops into Hanover. Russia seized all British ships in Russian ports, and every port from the North Cape to Gibraltar was closed against the British flag. Behind this combination was the brain of Napoleon.

The story of the battle is well known. The Danes fought stubbornly. The love of the fatherland and the flag, the split flag of old Denmark—the *Dannebrog*—a white cross on a red field, was stimulated by the poets of the day. Old memories were awakened of the days of Juel, Hvidfeldt, and Tordenskjold. Workmen, peasants from the farms, and merchants from the city hastened to enroll. The students of the university, a thousand strong, enlisted to a man. The Danish ships, supported by the shore batteries, lay in the shallow waters of the Sound. The attacking party had to navigate their ships through narrow and dangerous shoals. On the church towers and roofs hundreds of spectators watched the great fight. There was a dearth of seamen. In some of the vessels there was, so a Danish account narrates, only one sailor in twenty. These raw crews were kept at their drill throughout the night prior to the battle.

LARGE PORCELAIN BOWL.
Painted in colours and richly gilded. Dated 2 April 1801.
With inscription in memory of the brave Danes who fell at the Battle of Copenhagen
(*At Dansk Folke Museum, Copenhagen.*)

Writing to the *Times* in 1801, an officer present at the engagement says: "The enemy made a very obstinate resistance and fought like brave men. Most of our ships are very much cut up ... and the vessels which have been captured are perfect sieves, there being hardly a single plank in any one of them but has at least ten shot-holes in it. In fact, it was the most dreadfully fought action that ever took place in the annals of history." Of the shattered prizes, only one Danish vessel was fit to be repaired and taken to Portsmouth.

It was at this battle, as every schoolboy knows, that Nelson disregarded Admiral Parker's signal, "I have only one eye," he said, turning to his captain, "and may be allowed to be blind on occasion." Placing the spy-glass to his blind eye he said, "Upon my word, I do not see any signal."

A young Danish officer, a lad of seventeen, Villemoes, commanding a floating battery with twenty-four men, stuck to his post till only four of his men remained. Nelson, after the battle, begged the Crown Prince to introduce the young officer to him. The brave deeds of two great fighting races stand out on that day of awful carnage. Captain Larssen, after the battle, when he appeared in the streets of Copenhagen, was the object of universal homage as the hero of Bloody Maundy Thursday. When he passed Amagertorv, the fishwives would rise and make him a deep curtsy. Yet he passed his days in straitened circumstances and died well-nigh forgotten. No statue commemorates his memory.

But there is a ceramic record of that day of great battle. We illustrate a Copenhagen porcelain bowl, with painted scene, showing the *Dannebrog* flying and the sea-fight in progress. It was given, painted in colours, to the officers, and uncoloured to the *sous-officiers* who fought on the 2nd of April 1801. There is one at the *Dansk Folke Museum* and another at Rosenborg Castle, and the few other bowls in private hands are highly treasured as heirlooms. It is inscribed on a panel:—

Tilegnet
O. Fischer
og alle brave Danske.
Kiöbenhavn 2 April 1801,
af
Roepstorff.

(Dedicated to O. Fischer and all the brave Danes. Copenhagen, 2 April 1801, by Roepstorff.)

It is a sad story—the world-wide-empire dreams of one man had brought devastating ruin to friend and foe alike. There are many memories of the Battle of the Baltic; many links of friendship between the island kingdoms by the sea have been forged since then.

Let us think of them that sleep
Full many a fathom deep
By thy wild and stormy steep,
Elsinore!

Lord Nelson's Letters to Lady Hamilton.—The letters of Lord Nelson at that date have an interesting reference to Copenhagen porcelain. Apart from finding his portrait on Staffordshire earthenware mugs and jugs as a national hero, and commemorative of his victories, he took a considerable pleasure in ceramic art. In 1802 he ordered a Worcester service, pieces of which are found in the cabinets of collectors. His letters frequently contain references to his china, e.g.: "I send by the coach a little parcel containing the keys of the plate-chest and the case of the tea-urn, and there is a case of Colebrook Dale breakfast set and some other things."

CUP (1830-1840).
With view of Kronborg Castle, with shipping on the Sound.
Painted in colours and richly gilded.
(At Dansk Folke Museum, Copenhagen.)

After the Battle of Copenhagen one of his letters to Lady Hamilton is as follows:—

April 14, 1801.
My dear Friend,

I was in hopes that I should have got off some Copenhagen china to have sent you by Captain Bligh, who was one of my seconds on the 2nd. He is a steady seaman, and a good and brave man....

Another letter to Lady Hamilton, written on the following day, runs:—
St. George, April 15, 1801.
My dearest Friend,

I can get nothing here worth your acceptance, but as I know you have a valuable collection of china, I send you some of the Copenhagen manufacture. It will bring to your recollection that here your attached friend Nelson fought and conquered. Captain Bligh has promised to take charge of it, and I hope it will reach you safe....

Ever yours, most faithfully,
Nelson and Bronte.

At this date Müller had not retired from the factory, and Nelson undoubtedly procured some specimens of the best period. It is a matter of conjecture as to whether these examples are now known and in what collection in England they may be found.

Hardly had the echoes of the booming guns died away when Copenhagen was again bombarded by a British fleet in 1807, and the Danish fleet captured to prevent it falling into the hands of Napoleon. A fire had consumed a quarter of the city in 1795, and, succeeded by these later calamities, produced a condition of considerable distress and misery. The porcelain factory had its share of disaster. Falling bombs did irreparable damage: thousands of pounds' worth of porcelain and moulds were destroyed. This last blow was indeed a terrible one for the factory, and helped to complete its ruin.

PLATE.
 Painted with flower subject in natural colours overglaze by Jensen. Date 1827 Rich gilding at border with apparently experimental designs.
 Mark three lines and | in blue.
 (*At Museum, Royal Copenhagen Porcelain Factory.*)

 The so-called Empire Style.—But there came another Continental movement inimical to art in no less degree than war—the great inventive spirit which produced the age of machinery. Art grew impoverished and unfertile. Genius seemed to have descended on the workshop and the loom. The painter, the designer, the creator of forms, and the artist in colours lived in a nightmare of banalities. In regard to England, this industrial revolution has been a most powerful factor in stifling art. In Denmark, happily, this problem has not even yet come with overwhelming force, as there are no mines, no copper, iron, or coal, and the shadowy side of scientific invention and deadening commerce has not darkened the artistic horizon.

In considering the ceramics of Denmark, it should be borne in mind that, owing to an isolated northern position, artistic movements affecting the great European centres were slower in obtaining a foothold in Copenhagen. This in a great measure explains the steady growth of national art on its own lines. It was not until 1824, when G. Hetch became director, that the Copenhagen factory commenced to produce designs, then almost disappearing in other parts of Europe, in the Empire style.

Count Caylus in France and Winckelmann in Germany in middle eighteenth-century days had heralded the oncoming classic movement which had its *furore* of simplicity under the Empire.

Sir William Hamilton and Wedgwood had carried on the traditions in England. The Copenhagen factory at this date followed the decoration of Berlin and Vienna.

A Cup of this period (1830-1840) is illustrated (p. 185). This cup is heavily gilded in the prevalent atrocious style. It is finely painted in natural colours, having a marine scene representing the Castle of Kronborg, with the Sound, and a vessel in full sail. It was here on the ramparts that Hamlet met the ghost of his father. To-day the Danish soldiers in blue uniform keep sentry-go on the platform of the bastion. The bugle-call echoes across the Sound, and the grey frowning walls hold the mystery of the poet's dream.

One recalls Hamlet's vigil here, with his "The air bites shrewdly, it is very cold," and Horatio's reply, "It is a nipping and an eager air," and the angry waves beating below and the gathering storm from the north complete the picture.

We recollect the words—

The king doth wake to-night, and takes his rouse,
Keeps wassail, and the swaggering up-spring reels;
The kettle-drum and trumpet thus bray out
The triumph of his pledge.

And remembering, fall in a muse, to be aroused by the note of the bugle and the clash of arms of the guard.

FIGURE OF MERCURY.
After Thorvaldsen. White porcelain unglazed.

It was here that Charles XII of Sweden came with an army to lay siege, and the place where the manacled prisoners sat in the chapel is yet another link between yesterday and to-day. Here, too, is the tiny room, the prison of the young Queen Caroline Matilda, with barred window, overlooking the stormy sea.

The picture of Kronborg Castle on a cup conjures up a list of tragic memories. It is meet that it should find a record in Copenhagen porcelain. It is a page from Danish history.

Plates of this period show the heavy style that had descended on the factory. Deep gold bands enclose a circular picture, painted in a warm brown colour by Garmein about 1820-1825. They are mainly topographical in character. A plate painted by Jensen is signed with his initial, together with the three blue lines as a factory mark (illustrated, p. 189). It is a fine flower-subject in natural colours, representing primula, blue flowers, and daffodil. The border is richly gilded and has three distinct patterns; it evidently has been used as an experimental piece. It is now in the Museum at the royal factory. There are other plates painted in colours by L. Lyngbe, in 1831 and 1833 respectively, bearing his initial L. They are decorated in rich gilding by Brandstrup. One represents Söroe (with title on medallion), the Eton of Denmark. The other is of Prince's Palace, Christiansborg, Copenhagen.

The Thorvaldsen Period.—In 1867 the factory came under the control of A. Falck, and the director Holm, although not capable of raising the artistic output to its old level, introduced a new feature in a number of biscuit figures after Thorvaldsen, the great Danish sculptor.

We reproduce the well-known figure of the god *Mercury*, as indicating the beauty of these productions. Interesting as they are, and undoubtedly possessing great delicacy as replicas of masterpieces of another art, the decadent note is still present in denoting that the modellers had to seek inspiration elsewhere. It is pleasurable to be able to collect a miniature gallery of Thorvaldsen's work in porcelain, but the potting and modelling of them added nothing to the creative faculty of the artists at the factory.

The only productions of importance now conducted were an occasional jubilee or presentation vase made from Hetch's old moulds, decorated with a view of some villa or some edifice associated with the person who ordered the vase. They were usually covered with lilac or purple ground and profusely gilded.

The flame had not gone out, but it was flickering fitfully, and the artistic impulses in painting, and the poetry that had never died in Denmark, were stirring to kindle the fire into renewed life.

Since Höyen, the historian, delivered his lecture in 1844 *On the Conditions for the Development of a National Scandinavian Art*, artists had turned homewards. There was the national spirit of the northern people, the peasants and the fisher-folk, to make the Danish *genre* picture. There was nothing northern to be found in Rome. Eckersberg had indicated the way, and with the study of man came the study of nature. Johann Thomas Lunbye, with his cattle and his forest landscapes, caught the somnolent air of cattle before Troyon had set the fashion in France. Peter Christian Skovgaad interpreted the spiritual beauty of the Danish beech-woods; his favourite light was the cold pale day of the northern sky with its sober blue. Kroyer, with his *Skagen Fishers at Sunset*, and his *Fishermen setting out by Night*, surrounds the *Dansk Folke* with mystery and poetry.

To these days belong the rejuvenation of Danish art, and what the painter was doing on his canvas the ceramic artist was shortly to do on his vase and on his placque. The dawn of the Renaissance was at hand.

CHAPTER VIII

THE MODERN RENAISSANCE

CHAPTER VIII

THE MODERN RENAISSANCE

The after-effects of war—Philip Schou, Councillor of State, rebuilds the factory—Arnold Krog appointed art director—A new technique developed—Triumph of modern Copenhagen porcelain—The new impulses stimulate other European potters—A new note added to European ceramic art—The avoidance of classic or stereotyped styles—The idiosyncrasies of Copenhagen—Intense national sentiment of Copenhagen—Marks of leading painters and modellers.

On the threshold of the great Renaissance of art which re-established the name and fame of the Royal Copenhagen Factory, it is necessary to look at the subject from more than one point of view. The fire which Müller had lit had been burning dimly; indeed, save for the blue-and-white utilitarian ware, it had almost gone out. The Copenhagen factory was a century old in the seventies. Most of our English porcelain factories had put out their furnaces for ever. Chelsea, Derby, Plymouth, Bristol, and Bow had entered that ghostly realm where collectors snatch at the body of the potters and posterity portions out the inheritance of the departed great.

The years of the English porcelain factories, with their triumphs and their decadence, were compassed within the span of a man's life. Plymouth and Bristol, the only hard-paste factories, together ran less than twenty years. Bow succumbed in less than half a century. Chelsea existed only thirty-nine years, and Derby, with all its vicissitudes of fortune, changing hands many times, never reached a century old. The Worcester factory is the only English porcelain factory in existence to-day with a history which goes back to the middle years of the eighteenth century.

PLACQUE. WILD GEESE ON ICE.
Painted in underglaze colours by Arnold Krog. Period 1891-1895.

The half-century from 1825 to 1875, not only in Copenhagen but in every part of Europe, represents a dead level of banality in art. Sporadic attempts to awaken enthusiasm or to stimulate public interest fell on stony ground. Genius unrequited, and hardly recognized, consumed its life energy in solitary grandeur in many a lonely furrow. The period is bounded on the one side by the Napoleonic Wars, and on the other by the Crimean War and by the Franco-Prussian War. In England, artistic impulses were stifled by the rapid progress of the age of machinery, led by the Manchester school of thought— Ricardo and John Stuart Mill. A soil so sterile as this was incapable of producing the highest artistic results. The treasuries of many of the great European Powers had been drained almost to depletion by vital wars, and the little kingdom of Denmark had her share of political troubles. The war-cloud had settled on the isthmus of Schleswig-Holstein. Prussia and Austria and Denmark were whirled in a maelstrom of incessant warfare concerning the duchies of Schleswig-Holstein. All the Great Powers became involved. For forty years the struggle in one form or another broke out anew like a smouldering fire. It was not until 1866 that the Treaty of Vienna definitely assigned the future of the duchies to the Powers. This is not the place to discuss the rights and wrongs of a prolonged struggle by Denmark against more powerful neighbours, but in consequence of the widespread arena of conflict, from Missunde to Jutland, and the large war indemnity paid, it is manifest that the fine arts came very near extinction in such troublous times, when blow upon blow was rained upon the kingdom of Denmark.

The fortunes of the factory were at a low ebb, as we have seen in dealing with the decadent period. But in 1883 the models, stores, and other effects of the factory were sold to the limited company "Aluminia." From this date a new future commenced for the factory.

Philip Schou rebuilds the Factory.—The hour demanded the man, and the man was Philip Schou, who came as the pioneer of modernity. In the outskirts of the capital, close to the park of the Castle of Frederiksberg, large buildings were erected, containing workshops provided with the latest improvements in machines and kilns of the newest designs. The ovens were much larger than the older type, and designed to hold about 15,000 pieces of average size. These drastic changes at the dawn of the Renaissance, entirely due to the foresight of Schou, necessitated the expenditure of a considerable amount of money. It is not surprising to find that during the first years the undertaking, from a financial point of view, did not prove successful. This, at the time, except to Schou, may not have been recognized as the happiest omen, but it is a postulate that art and commercialism do not usually thrive together. It was the same in Müller's day; it has always been an admitted fact, and it always will be acknowledged that the cloven hoof of commercialism has marked the oncoming of a decadent period. But Philip Schou had ambitions and desires which no reverses could thwart. His practical grasp of the situation and his perspicacious conception of future possibilities, which have now been realized, stamp him as a man possessed of that rare combination of poetry and practicability which marks the pioneer of any great enterprise.

PLACQUE.
With autumnal scene painted in underglaze colours. By Arnold Krog. Period 1896-1900.

There are triumphs of great business organization which compel our admiration in no less degree than artistic achievements won in equally adverse conditions. To build up the decayed fortunes of a moribund art, to combat financial disaster and impending ruin, require indomitable courage and intensity of application which cannot be classed other than as genius.

The great period of Müller and the great triumphs were sinking into oblivion. Of the once famous factory it seemed as though little might be left but the name. The old models of beautiful symmetry had long been set aside or even destroyed. The favourite blue-and-white service, the national pattern treasured as the remaining heirloom, had lost all its style and harmony. Haphazard conditions prevailed and slovenly results predominated. Originality had taken wing and deserted the old factory. The old mussel design was painted on any form that found its way into Denmark from other factories.

Copenhagen was content to follow, and leave art and prestige to take care of themselves. Now and again artistic productions, such as a wedding or a jubilee vase made from the old moulds, like milestones, marked the road. With this material, with its poverty of art and paucity of ideas, the new director, shrewd and energetic, saw that no headway could be made. A demand for artistic and original decoration of articles of domestic use and luxury was just making itself felt, and there was some talk of creating a national Christian VI style. But the factory has accomplished something greater—it has created a European style.

The early days of the factory, with its new impulses and its youthful spirit of modernity, are reflected at once in the first attempts to inaugurate something of artistic and permanent value. The comparison between Schou and Müller holds good in many respects. They both were men in advance of their day. They were builders, not only in the sense of being pioneers of an artistic industry, but in the practical sense of laying down ovens and expending money on valuable plant as a means to the great end they had in view. The struggle against adversity, the accumulating cloud of financial losses, the want of outside support, are common factors in both these men's sturdy fight against failure. Müller had to combat the inheritance of failure left by Fournier, and Philip Schou had to overcome the deathly inertia that had paralysed the factory during the decadence. It is not easy to find co-operation in face of a general tendency in an opposite direction. Mediocre minds find it more congenial to float unconcernedly with the stream. Schou was the strong swimmer fighting against the current.

There is one other point where he claims kinship with Müller; he was felicitous in the selection of his lieutenants, and his choice of artistic assistance to further his ambitions was as wise as it was phenomenally prescient.

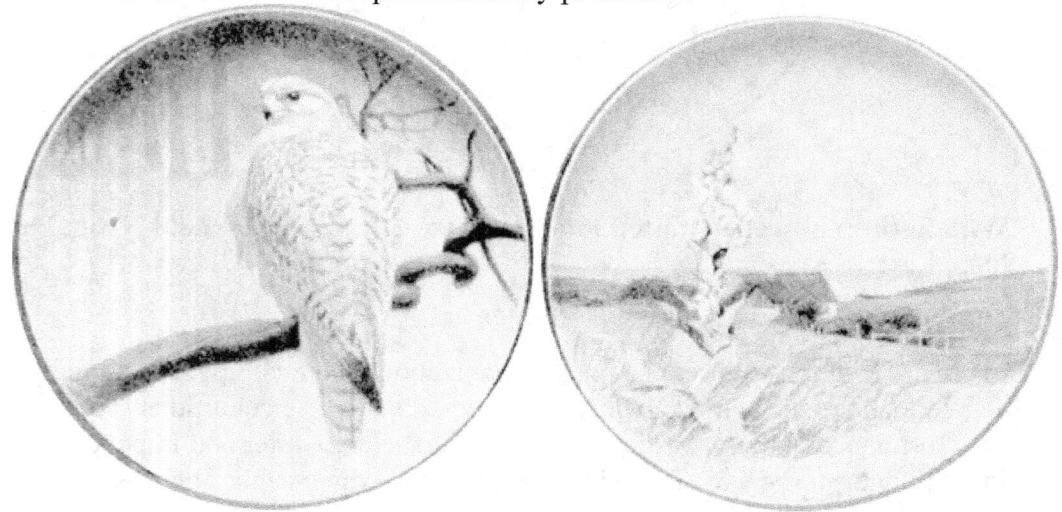

PLACQUES.
Painted in underglaze colours. Diameter 9 inches.
Kestrel by V. Th. Fischer.
Meadow with farmhouse by C. F. Liisberg.

Arnold Krog appointed Art Director.—In 1885 Arnold Krog became an artist at the factory. Trained as an architect and a painter, he had already spent five years in the restoration of Frederiksborg Castle, and like those old Italian craftsmen who made all art their domain, he came to the decoration of porcelain with instinctive appreciation of its qualities.

A happier combination than this could not have been desired. Schou, the business head, the man of strength of purpose, tenacity of will, battling with stern facts and figures, and Arnold Krog, the artist and dreamer, inventing new forms, wrestling with technical problems with a practical skill wedded to poetic impulses.

The days of early Renaissance were filled with eager incessant work, and whatever difficulties surged up to the doors of the factory, Schou resisted them bravely. He believed in the future of the factory, he believed in the work of the artists. It was this great proud belief of a great man in his life's work that created the second great period in the history of the Royal Copenhagen Porcelain Factory. This quotation from a fellow-worker of that date shows how lovingly his memory is still cherished: 'Optimistic and broad-minded man as he was, he firmly believed that the factory would succeed in spite of all difficulties. He did not look for immediate profit, but left us to work in peace, undisturbed by all the anxieties and pecuniary difficulties with which he, as managing director, must have had to contend."

A New Technique developed.—In regard to the direction in decoration which the new porcelain took, it is interesting to realize how distinct a departure this was from contemporary art. The moment that Arnold Krog awakened to the fact that the body of the porcelain is smooth, white, hard, and of surpassing beauty, that moment determined its future. To cover it with colours or with gold in the overglaze style, as his predecessors had done, was at once to extinguish its innate loveliness. If blue dots and lines could be painted on plates, surely, thought the new art director, other artistic designs could be produced in the same manner. From these premises the principle of underglaze painting was accepted, and has been since followed so successfully.

The determination of the method employed immediately led to the inquiry as to the exact definition such painting was to take. The difficulty now was to decide what to paint. It was obvious that mere ornamentation would lead to nothing new. Could Europe teach Copenhagen anything? It apparently could, at that stage. Accordingly, Philip Schou and Arnold Krog made a tour of Holland, Belgium, France, and England, and visited many of the leading factories. At the Antwerp Exhibition they saw many beautiful things from Sèvres and the other great European factories, but they had to admit that their journey was in a great measure fruitless, as they did not discover what they sought—new impulses for original work.

It was not enough that all traditional arabesques and scrolls should be discarded: the plain white resplendent surface of the ware demanded its place in the scheme of decoration.

At Paris, Arnold Krog visited the collection of M. S. Bing, who had just returned with rich treasures of Oriental art from China and Japan. These masterpieces in bronze, earthenware, porcelain, and ivory, together with drawings and colour-prints with endless variety of composition, brought with them an atmosphere of ancient culture, artistic genius, and unerring instinct, and to the mind capable of unlocking the mysteries of the old unexplored East they revealed their secret.

The immediate results indicate clearly enough that Copenhagen had not "jumped a claim" and found treasure-trove upon which she could live till others gained the secret. There was no slavish imitation of the designs of the Oriental potter, as was the case with Sèvres and with Worcester. With true vision, the results of the East were traced to the original source of inspiration, and henceforth Nature in all her forms, in all her varying phases and moods, became the mirror into which Copenhagen looked to see herself reflected.

With such an ideal before the factory there was work enough for all and much to be accomplished. The records of this period show the incessant labours of all concerned in building anew the fortunes of the factory. Liisberg the sculptor was appointed modeller, and a young apprentice, Hallin, was made his assistant. The extreme difficulty of the technique offered frequent disappointments. The tone is determined by the exact thickness of the layer of pigment applied, and it is impossible to distinguish between the different shades before the firing has taken place. The only guide in this work is a fine instinct. But the enthusiasm of the little band of workers, modellers and artists, was not damped by the vagaries of the furnace. With little enough by way of precedent to guide them, they attained a sure and unerring technique and a complete mastery over the idiosyncrasies of the medium in which they worked. These early years of intense application have created traditions for the factory, and the days of Philip Schou stand as never to be forgotten in the strenuous outburst of initiative industry which has raised a monument to Danish handicraft and culture. In 1902 Philip Schou resigned his position as managing director, and it is pleasurable to record that in a full and complete life he has seen his early dreams realized. He received decoration at the hands of foreign Governments, and in 1888 was made a knight-commander of the Legion of Honour. Copenhagen porcelain had won European distinction, being acclaimed as adding new impulses and teaching a new technique to the older factories.

PLACQUES.
Painted in underglaze colours. Diameter 9 inches.
Bird subject by V. Th. Fischer.
Cow in meadow at edge of lake by G. Rode.

The early successes of the porcelain were as surprising to the leading experts of Europe as they were gratifying to the pioneers of the Copenhagen Renaissance. It is an interesting fact that the first piece painted in underglaze colours was bought in September 1885 by the Duke of Sutherland, whose yacht was lying in the Sound. The Duke paid a visit to the royal factory, and although at that time only three pieces were finished, he carried off a specimen decorated with a stork flying over a lake. Such an historic piece as this is now worth a considerable sum.

Triumph of Modern Copenhagen Porcelain.—At the great International Exposition at Paris in 1889, the Royal Copenhagen exhibit attracted unusual attention. Although the factory was not then in a position to make a grand show of large or costly pieces, French collectors and connoisseurs besieged the show-cases, and the demand far exceeded the supply, ten times the price asked being offered in many instances by disappointed collectors. Within fourteen days of the opening of the Exhibition everything of any artistic value was sold. Coupled with this commercial success came the award of the *Grand Prix d'honneur*, a rare distinction at that time, especially for so small an undertaking.

At this Exhibition the coloured crystalline glazes were shown for the first time. These, now so well known in the adoption by most of the leading factories of the world, were discovered in 1886 by Clement, the chemist at the Royal Copenhagen Factory, and perfected by his successor, Hr. Engelhardt. (This crystalline ware is dealt with separately in Chapter X.)

The days of the early Renaissance were full of promise—a promise that has not been unfulfilled. The old factories, with traditions of a century and a half, threw off their lethargy at the trumpet-blast of modernity. The Copenhagen factory was like the fairy prince of the romantic tale who blew the magic horn and awakened the sleeping princesses.

The New Impulses stimulate other European Potters.—Art criticism of this period abounds in glowing tribute. M. Edouard Garnier, one of the directors of the Sèvres factory, wrote in the *Gazette des Beaux Arts* in 1889: "Not one of the foreign porcelain factories which in 1878 threatened to become dangerous rivals to us seems to have made any progress; on the other hand, the beautiful exhibits of the Royal Porcelain Factory of Copenhagen are quite a revelation to us: they show quite a new spirit in the art of porcelain-making."

Among the varied developments at this time considerable attention was given to the form of the blue-and-white "mussel"-painted ware, and a wonderful variety of shapes followed each other in quick succession. All the old artificial and oftentimes meaningless designs which had crept in during the decadent period were discarded, and were replaced by tasteful and natural designs which were conceived with a view to the characteristic lines in their decoration. The great and wonderful inventiveness and rich variety of this table ware in its thousand forms are therefore the consummation of the incessant search for truth and symmetry and beauty which characterized the early Renaissance period.

PLACQUE.
Painted in underglaze colours, by C. Liisberg. Diameter 12 inches.

If proof be needed of the great influence Copenhagen art exercised on contemporary ceramics, the proof is ready to hand. Just eleven years after the Paris Exposition of 1889 came the great Exposition of 1900, and an examination of the *grand-feu* specimens of the Sèvres factory shows to what extent the delicate tones of the new Copenhagen technique in underglaze painting had affected the French potters. Crystalline glazes had by this time been developed. In 1894 M. Edouard Garnier, of the National factory at Sèvres, in again passing judgment upon the work of Copenhagen, refers to the fact that two specimens exhibiting "marvellous skill in the execution"—the *Flight of the Sparrows* and the *Lilacs*—were bought for inclusion in the modern collection of ceramic art of the Sèvres Museum, and to this museum Hr. Philip Schou sent the first specimens of varied colorations "*au grand feu*" and the experiments made by Hr. Engelhardt of full or partial crystallized glazes.

In regard to the general atmosphere of the *grand-feu* ceramics, the Sèvres factory had by 1900, the year of the Exhibition, turned with such fond eyes to Copenhagen that the results then offered, triumphs though they were, reflected something more than usual of the Northern spirit. For instance, one remembers the two great biscuit groups in hard porcelain for table decoration at the Élysée, by Frémiet, the master sculptor. These were 4 feet 8 inches in height, and were marvels of fabrication. The one was the Athenian *Minerva*, and the other the Scandinavian *Diana* standing in her chariot, with a hound at her feet and driving two reindeer. These were the first pieces of so great a size ever made in biscuit at Sèvres. Figures of Northern animals followed the success of the factory by the Baltic, and there was one, a *Wolf* tracing human steps in the snow, by M. Valton, which won commendation. Nor was this all. The grey tones were successfully reproduced in the *Danish Dogs*, by Gardet.

There is no greater tribute to pay to the inspiring genius behind the Royal Copenhagen Factory than to enumerate these instances of old factories with the prestige of Sèvres and Meissen hailing the newly awakened spirit of a younger factory. On every side, in these days, came the tribute of praise generously given by masters of technique and by rival workers in art. The Renaissance was something more than a name—it had become an accomplished fact.

The great achievement of the modern Renaissance period is the creation of a new technique in underglaze decoration, which has added something to modern European ceramic art. The underglaze blue, employed at the old royal factory by Müller, was familiar from early Meissen days. But the revelation that underglaze painting of landscape had become something more romantic than Chinese prototypes was a fact only realized after Copenhagen had made successful experiment. The landscape of the Oriental potter, at the best, had something of formality and followed a convention alien to Western laws of perspective. Differing essentially from the enamel colours of the overglaze Continental work, and not less so from the glost-kiln colours of the English factories in their underglaze work, the *grand-feu* colours, with their scheme of harmonies imparted something fresh and original to the art of the modern potter.

It is, therefore, of great interest, commingled with considerable speculation, to contemplate the various stages of evolution of this characteristic style, and to await the future phases of its development.

In reviewing the work of this Renaissance period, an attempt has been made by the writer to arrive at some conclusion as to that exact point of time at which the genius of the factory reaches its whitest heat during a brilliant quarter of a century of work. In a rich field of design which exhibits so much character and freshness, when new surprises may come forth from the oven at any moment, no inconsiderable difficulty presents itself in selecting any period where the work is more excellent.

Happily, in contemplating the underglaze productions of Copenhagen, there is an extended period which may be passed in review. It is perhaps natural, when making tests of the general output of work, to select the middle years as productive of ceramic art of the highest order. There is the advantage in point of date of being able to apply a standard to it, either side by side with earlier work, or in comparison with later creations in the same style of decoration by the same band of artists and modellers.

The number and character of the decorative pieces produced at the Royal Copenhagen Porcelain Factory during the ten years from 1896 to 1905, to which the highest praise has been given, seem to indicate that a close investigation of the details of the work of the individual modellers and artists might with advantage be pursued by those cosmopolitan collectors intent on acquiring masterpieces representative of the highest modern ceramic art.

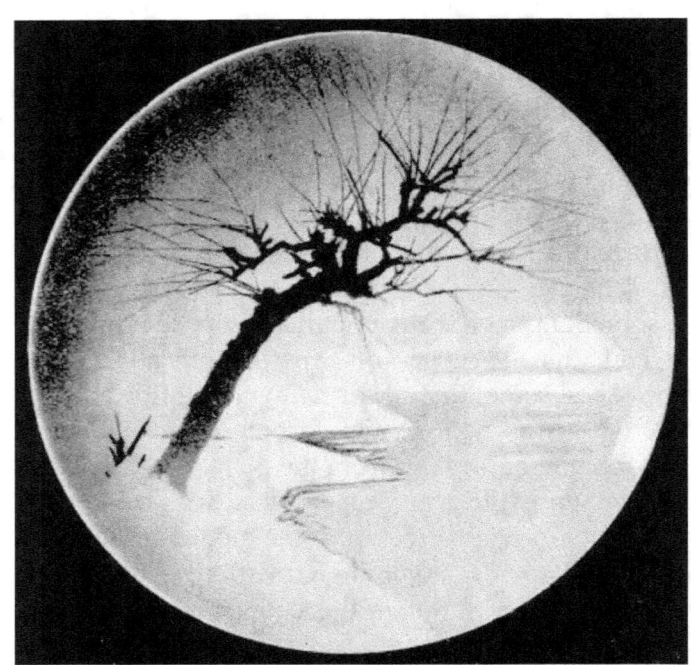

PLACQUE. SNOW SCENE WITH SETTING SUN.
Painted in underglaze colours. Signed A. Smidth.

Personal tastes and predilections are not unimportant factors in passing judgment upon the present-day work of the factory, but the authorities of museums in various parts of the world, whose standard is a high one, have not hesitated in selecting modern examples of Royal Copenhagen porcelain. In following the trend of the development of the porcelain since the great outburst in 1900, when at the Paris Exhibition by general acclamation Copenhagen was acknowledged to be ahead of all other European factories, disinterested critics and less disinterested competitors have eagerly watched the progress of the Danish ware. Art requires no passport to cross international barriers, and foreign experts have enthusiastically admitted that the work of Copenhagen is of surprising beauty. At successive exhibitions, when nation has stood in friendly rivalry with nation, the ceramic record of Copenhagen has not been dimmed by equal work. So far it is still in advance of every one in Europe. Imitators it has, and, as the old adage puts it, "imitation is the sincerest form of flattery."

The question is always asked of factories "with a past," whether it be Sèvres or Meissen, Wedgwood or Worcester—Is the work of to-day an echo of past glories, has the lamp burned dim, is the sacred fire still alight? In regard to other factories this is not the place to make any pronouncement, nor is it impossible to say that at any moment the spirit of the presiding genius of these great factories with great traditions may awaken to inspire anew the modern potters upon whom the mantle of succession has fallen. To cover European factories in a survey is often to come upon silent and deserted temples with decrepit worshippers offering sacrifices to a dim and distant past. But the oracle may yet speak.

It is here that Copenhagen, with its great period of overglaze work, under the Müller *régime*, holding equality with the great factories of its day, as we have shown in earlier chapters, now comes forward with a second great period of underglaze work, bearing no immediate relationship with the first. Holger Danske has awakened to give magic potency to the Danish art.

The following are the chief characteristics of Royal Copenhagen porcelain. It is always hard fired *au grand feu*, and the various classes of the underglaze decorated ware may be summarized as follows:—

Underglaze Painted

I. *Individual Pieces.*

Vases and placques signed by the artists who have painted them. Such unique specimens of personal work are never reproduced.

(A list of artists, with facsimile reproductions of their signatures, will be found at the end of this chapter.)

II. *General Art Objects.*

Vases, placques, bibelots, and ornamental subjects.

These are designed with a view to general production, and this practice has originated since 1893.

PLACQUE.
With geese and landscape painted in underglaze colours. Signed C. F. Liisberg.

In this class may be included the collection of Commemorative Placques designed by Arnold Krog. The number struck of these is limited, and they are never repeated after the occasion for which they were made (see p. 243).

More strictly utilitarian ware is represented by the continuous output of the blue-and-white fluted service, to which new forms are constantly being added.

III. *Figure Subjects.*

Peasants, children, and animal life—quadrupeds, birds, and fish—all modelled directly from nature.

IV. *Vases and Modelled Subjects with Coloured or Crystallized Glazes.*

This style was commenced at Copenhagen as early as 1886, and is described in detail, Chapter X.

Overglaze Painted Porcelain

Revival of porcelain in the style of the Juliane Marie period, modelled and decorated from old and rare examples. This is the latest phase of development.

In tabulated form some conception may be formed as to the classes into which the work of the modern Renaissance may be divided. Something must be said about the immediate causes which directed the line of progression and advancement in the course it has taken.

The principles of decoration especially applying to porcelain, smooth, white, and hard, such as this, have been realized to the full by Arnold Krog, the art director of the factory.

The uttermost developments of the underglaze painting are governed by the axiom that such a fine body as that of the Copenhagen porcelain is instantly destroyed by being covered with colours or with gilding. The old Danish mussel-blue painted underglaze dinner ware is the skeleton upon which the fabric of the modern Renaissance movement has been built.

The Avoidance of Classic or Stereotyped Styles.—Something of the forcefulness of the originality of Copenhagen may be gathered from a brief hypothetical survey of what divergent paths design might have taken even at that critical moment when it was determined to employ the underglaze colours for decorative landscape subjects. The conventional panel might have been still employed, and with it the formal scenes of gardens with cavaliers and ladies, bringing the Chinese landscape subject into Western perspective, and at the same time eschewing the vivid colours of Sèvres or Meissen. Or underglaze painting, in blue and the other *grand-feu* colours, might have found itself in panels supplemented by overglaze enamel colours of bright tone, in floral decoration, or *œil-de-perdrix* and other luscious patterns, and richly gilded. It might, not unnaturally, have appeared to be a safer beginning to develop the Danish conventional pattern into something more intricate in design, with geometrical borders and formal floral painting or with old Scandinavian interlaced designs of Runic character, exhibiting the newer advance of underglaze treatment.

Copenhagen, with wise rejection, took none of these courses, and the Renaissance leapt into being not only with new applications of underglaze painting, but with a complete and rapidly perfected theory wherein the subject became a ceramic poem. Throwing all convention to the winds, it brought tone to underglaze painting, and within the limits of the potter's technique, the same relative atmospheric quality to the decorated vase or placque as there is on the canvas of the painter.

The porcelain found itself in an incredibly short time, and rapidly passed through its initial stages. The first light had come from the East. The influx into Europe of some of the finest art work of Japan had a marked effect on design.

But Krog's genius was too original to snatch at the body; he caught the spirit of the best, and the first attempts have a slight indication of their origin, till with full strength Copenhagen needed no guiding hand to lead her to the inspiration of all true design. The simple forms of nature were translated into ceramic art, and the melting, dreamy, sad-hued porcelain was imbued with the subtle effects of the Danish landscape. The great simplicity of *motif* was the great simplicity of genius. The effects are so natural and reticent that their greatness might well escape common observation. But the trained eyes of half the potters in Europe and of connoisseurs of the highest ceramic art were turned, and are turned still, to the output of the Copenhagen factory. *Summa ars est celare artem* is eminently applicable to the art of Arnold Krog and the band of Danish artists trained under him. There is nothing showy or clever, nothing cheap or meretricious in all their work. Everything that has come from Krog's hands has been well conceived, and an honest attempt made not to win admiration but to make one step forward in artistic evolution towards the ideal. Without seeking reward he has won the esteem of the cultured critics of a whole continent.

The Idiosyncrasies of Copenhagen.—Wherein lies the strength of Copenhagen porcelain? The mysteries of underglaze did not originate in Denmark. The blue, greenish-yellow, brown, sea-green, maroon, lemon-colour, celadon-green, and red, are colours found painted under the glaze in old Chinese examples in collections in various European museums. But there is a difference. Chinese landscapes in blue have a charm and atmosphere of their own, although the European taste has shown a marked preference for enamel-painted porcelain of more brilliant colours. The underglaze of the East was mainly confined to decorative conventional treatment. There is the exquisite family of jars, designed as presents at the New Year, painted underglaze, with the prunus blossom, and geometric pattern representing the breaking ice. These are grotesquely termed "ginger jars" in the jargon of the auction-room, and fine specimens bring immense prices under the hammer. In a measure these, and vases and beakers with floral decoration, and cups and saucers, with dragons or with the well-known "aster" pattern, may be regarded as conventional. From these prototypes Meissen and Sèvres and Worcester drew many fine inspirations.

In underglaze blue painting there is another class with landscapes and figures, such as bowls, of which there are infinite variety, which convey, in lieu of regular ornament, a certain atmosphere. Even the ordinary ginger jar of commerce, if it be old enough, exhibits a most alluring suggestiveness. These designs appear to be traditional on common ginger jars half a century apart in point of time. There is a background of mountains, and stretch of sky with a triangular flight of birds, flying high. There is a tree in the foreground, and a rustic homestead. On a bank a fisherman casts a line into the water, and away on the expanse of lake stands a junk. The whole is crudely and hastily drawn, and one jar, if not exactly the counterpart of another, has the same details in the scene. But, curiously enough, there is a poetry and depth of tone about these common ginger jars which is difficult to define.

To arrive at a technical reason for these differences in styles is to examine the theories governing the art of ceramics. To take the overglaze painting; this may be compared to the canvas of the painter which is covered with pigment. His sky is blue or red or yellow or an admixture of all three; the reflections of light on the water are touches of pigment. There is no part of the canvas over which his deft brush has not travelled. The underglaze painter on porcelain is like the etcher, who obtains his illumination from the uncovered surface of the copper upon which he works. The untouched portion of the plate of the etcher forms the wide expanse of sky, and gives luminosity to the deeply bitten lines of his subject. Similarly, in underglaze painting on porcelain, the dazzling white expanse of the body, afterwards to be coated with limpid transparent glaze, is the background into which the design of the artist must imperceptibly melt. It is this depth of tone and atmosphere which give poetic charm to underglaze painting.

But the *subject* is not left to take care of itself. Without pictorial indefinition the work may still remain on the plain of formal decoration even though that be superlatively conceived and executed.

VASE.
Painted in underglaze colours by V. Th. Fischer. Height 13 inches.

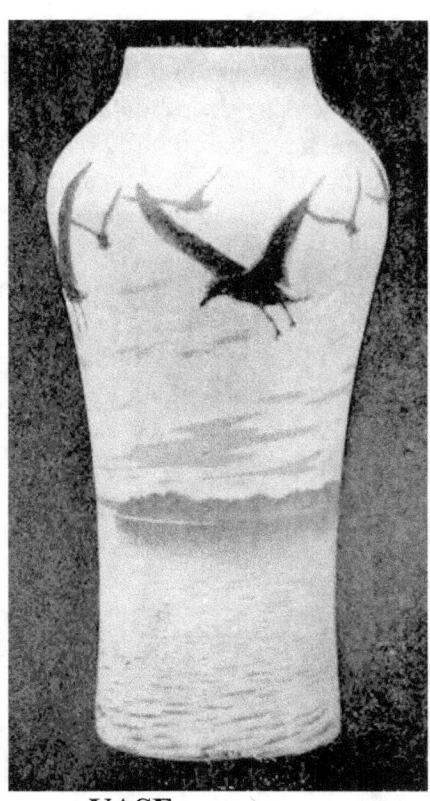

VASE.
Painted in underglaze colours by C. Liisberg. Height 20 inches.

What is it that one sees when one comes face to face for the first time with a Copenhagen vase of this golden period? The merest dilettante in porcelain-collecting must at once recognize something that he will find nowhere else in his cabinets. In form there is always, necessarily, a full expanse to carry the subject, if it be landscape. Nor is there a front and a reverse, as in the old school of conventionally treated landscapes circumscribed by panels. There is a breadth and continuity of subject traversing the circumference of the vase, which, from new points of view, offers new surprises.

The body is white and hard and of ivory-like closeness when seen by transmitted light. The rich liquid glaze has a slight greenish tone and has a surface like polished crystal. The quality of this glaze is exceptionally fine and possesses artistic properties peculiarly its own. In modelled subjects such as fish this is especially noticeable. In the noble figure of a *Sea Lion*, this glaze simulates the original so skilfully that the sensation conveyed is exactly that of the smooth, sleek, satin-like texture of that animal's body. It is obvious that with such a vehicle as this glaze the effects produced in landscape painting are those seen in nature in the sun-pierced vaporous haze of a climate remarkable for its exquisite tones.

In colour the subjects appear in low tones of subtle elusiveness, never, by reason of the technique of the underglaze palette, departing from the strictly limited range of colours we have enumerated. The tones of all these are pitched in a minor key. The brilliance of the painter in enamel is conspicuously absent. There is no scarlet, or bright yellow, or mazarin blue, or vivid green. The charm of colour lies in its exquisite delicacy.

It is the highest ceramic landscape painting offered to the delectation of those possessed of sufficient connoisseurship to appreciate the supreme handling of a difficult technique.

It departs from the Chinese prototypes in underglaze blue. The deep blue of Nankin is delightful in its poetry, but it is a convention that landscapes are painted all blue. Copenhagen becomes more realistic, but no less poetical, with added touches of amber, and mauve, and grey, and sage green, and the blue, pale and tender, carries out a colour scheme which stamps this Western art as something original and ideal.

It is thus seen that in body and glaze and colouring Copenhagen has excellent points challenging comparison with anything that has gone before. But with these technical problems solved satisfactorily, there is yet something to be added, which has created a reflective school of design and elevated Copenhagen to its present status. This quality, difficult to describe, and yet ever-present in the results when submitted to definite criticism, may be roughly summarized as consisting of two essential traits of disciplined art—the apt choice of decorative subject and the complete mastery exercised in fittingly decorating the object.

DECORATIVE MEMORIAL PLACQUE.
By Arnold Krog.
Commemorating the restoration of Ribe Cathedral, Denmark.

Apart from the technical excellence of selection of idea and symmetrical incorporation with the form under decoration, there is the national spirit, which is the soul imparted to the work of artists filled with intense love of nature. This charm, lightly and daintily woven into the dreams which the porcelain conveys in dim mysterious manner, cannot be captured by the snare of the imitator.

The Western potter hitherto had not quite realized that he must be a poet as well as a potter. To study Copenhagen porcelain is to read poetry conveyed in another medium than printing-ink and paper. Nor is this new of the highest ceramic art. To contemplate old Chinese porcelain is not to think in poetry but to speak in poetry. Great potters have twin souls the world over. The Chinese themselves have terms for their own ware which indicate the plane on which all great ceramic art should stand. To one colour is given the term "the moonlight," to another "the blue of the prune skin," to another "the violet of the wild apple," to another "the liquid dawn," to yet another "the red of the bean blossom." Descriptions of certain ware and certain colours and glazes become little poems, such as the account of the Ch'ai Yao—"As blue as the sky, as clear as a mirror, as thin as paper, and as resonant as a musical stone of jade." Nor is Chinese literature wanting in reiterated allusions to the beauty of the national porcelain. The wine cups are likened to "disks of thinnest ice" or to "tilted lotus leaves floating down a stream."

The strain of poetry, so pronouncedly a feature in modern Copenhagen work, is noticeable even in the old overglaze decorated porcelain. The innate love of nature found expression in its refusal to follow stereotyped forms of ceramic decoration. The national note never departed except during the decadence. The *Flora Danica* service, with its stiff and painstaking decorations in botanical style, was a monument to national ceramic art. The modern spirit, with its landscape and realism, is crystallized in a great gallery of placques and vases, and may be said to embody the *Poetica Danica*—the new interpretation of nature. The flowers are no longer botanical specimens pressed between the pages of a ceramic album. They are painted *in situ*, and become delicate units in dream pictures, beside still lakes or embosomed in grassy dells.

Intense National Sentiment of Copenhagen Style.—The Renaissance period is at once national and reflective of the moods of the land of its origin. The illustrations appearing in this chapter faintly suggest the luminosity of the originals, but in their selection an attempt has been made to show that a certain ordered progress has been at work. The earlier examples are significant of the lingering traces of Oriental suggestion, rapidly and completely assimilated, and any mannerism, if such there be, was pushed aside by the native growth of vigorous inventiveness and the rich profusion of forms and designs not dependent on any outside influence.

To compare Japanese art with that of Copenhagen is to compare two parallel lines which only meet in infinity and never coincide. Truth and sincerity, love of nature, and mastery of form are common to the Japanese and the Danish ceramists. But the former reflect the brilliance of colour harmonies of a land teeming with rich colour and steeped in Oriental tradition. The mirror is held to national life and sentiment, and accordingly movement, humour, poetry, are essentials in Japanese pottery.

The art of Copenhagen equally reflects the national life and character under a northern sky. Pensive, dreamy, tinged with the stillness of the Arctic night, with its violet sky, the wistful art of the North never attempts the sensuous moments of the art of the Far East. The beauty of form is reticent and reposeful. The range of the *grand-feu* colours coincides exactly with the tender colours of the little kingdom, and the melting glaze adds that luminosity which makes the Danish landscape so *spirituelle*.

Danish art has never attempted to be Japanese; on the other hand, Japan has seriously realized that the art of Copenhagen is worth the copying, and has done this with a light heart.

Again and again one is struck with the originality of a design new to ceramic decoration. The *Placque*, of the period 1896 to 1900 (illustrated, p. 207), is a case in point, and is almost the only instance of a dallying with the romantically artificial. But the effect is so charming and so poetical that it disarms criticism. What could promise so little as a subject for decorative treatment? A pair of iron gates, flanked with stone pillars surmounted by formal urns. An avenue of poplars approached by the ascending steps of a terrace, stretching from the foreground in two converging lines, with the solitary figure of a woman in black in the middle distance. That is all. But the result is an alluring picture of an old-world chateau. A touch of Southern elegance and courtly grace makes itself evident in the formal scene, with its pathos of the figure symbolizing lonely sorrow and the dark shadow of the chapel at the end of the grove.

It is possible, without eliminating much, to trace the steady growth of temperamental art during a quarter of a century in successive stages of five years. True to first impelling motives, the art of the factory has never turned back. The modern movement known as *l'art nouveau*, which swept across Europe with its meaningless swirls and curves, left no trace on the work of the Royal Copenhagen Factory. Rich in the possession and eager in the fulfilment of its own original conceptions, it had no need of extraneous impulses, and has remained unstirred by ephemeral art movements. The illustrations in this chapter are arranged chronologically as far as possible, and it will be seen that the subjects become as Danish as the ballad of King Christian. The gallery is rich in its dreamy suggestiveness, the ceramic record of reposeful scenes luxuriating in luscious somnolence—the sea, the sand-dunes, the wild swans, and geese, and mallards, the wood with its deer and wild life, the secluded lake with its denizens, the meadows, and the cattle of the farm lands.

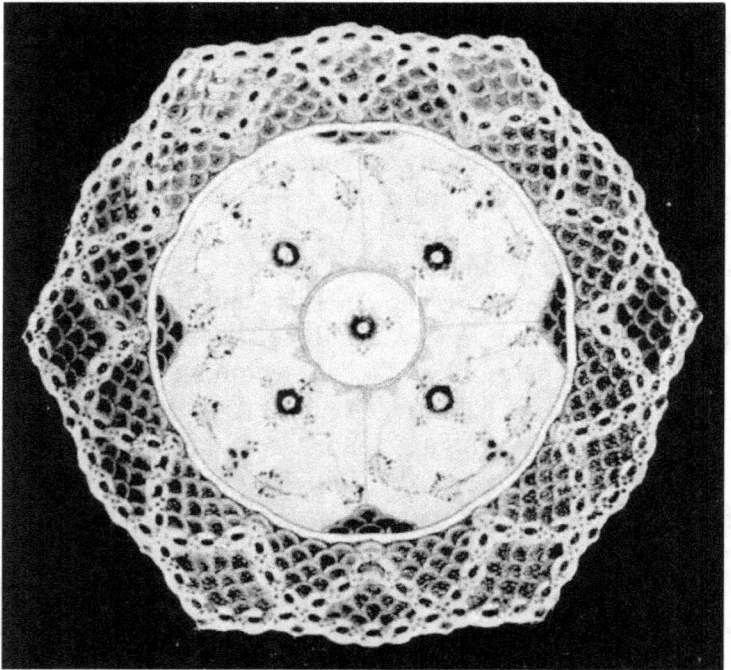

DESSERT PLATE.
With perforated border and rim decorated with scale design in blue, and having national Danish pattern in centre.

There has been a process of fermentation going on in modern Danish pictorial art, and its influence is seen on the porcelain produced at the royal factory. It is new because it is everlastingly old—the worship of Nature. There is in modern Copenhagen porcelain the tender, dreamy melancholy of the old Danish ballads. It is like some magic story told in the twilight. Everything is silent, nebulous, steeped in fragrant yet pathetic memories. There is a subtle and refined introspection, an æsthetic yearning akin to sadness.

Every Dane remembers Jacobsen's whimsical visionary Mogens, who hums softly to himself the refrain—"*I Längsel, I Längsel jeg lever!*" (Longing, longing I live!).

This tristful ideality is a note in literature not far to seek. The Danish poets have reflected Nature's moods with throbbing ecstasy, tinged with sombre forebodings. It comes with unexpected pathos as an ending to Christian Winther's poem *En Vandrer* (A Wanderer), who, after a pilgrimage through woodland glades of summerland, exclaims at the sight of the cloud-capped mountains in the distance—

Og—naar de er bestegne
Imorgen—ak!—hvad saa?

(And when they are climbed, to-morrow, alas! what then?)

The outlook of the Copenhagen potter-artists reflects the genius of inspired vision. The face of Nature is transfigured. This interpretation links poesy and pensive art indissolubly together in these ceramic poems palpitating with sensitiveness.

A touch of tender melancholy pervades the art of the potter. He has caught the pale green of the sea, the vibrating light on the long sand dunes and the silvery vaporous clouds that fret the horizon. To take a Copenhagen vase with its sea-scape and dancing spray and pack of scudding storm-clouds, tempts one to place it to one's ear as children do sea-shells; surely one shall hear the sound of the leaping surge and the roll of the breakers!

Bathed in liquid light, that soft effulgence peculiar to Denmark, where the sunlight is so soft and subdued and nothing stands out in harsh contrast, the scenery lends itself to soothing reverie. It has been given to few to commune with Nature in her melting moods, "like Niobe all tears." Corot stands for all time as having pierced the veil, and Cazin has caught the quivering play of ghostly light rarely made known to mortals. The modern Copenhagen potters have, "daring greatly," communed with Nature in like manner. They have essayed to "snatch a grace beyond the reach of art"—or of ceramic art. But success is theirs. The transparent atmosphere lending a pearly tone to the trembling stretches of soft verdure and the cool limpid shadows resting on the still meres are reflected in the porcelain. The pictures are soothing and restful; we can hear the flutter of the mallards among the reeds.

Of the *paysage intime* there is profusion of wealth in the long vista of the low-lying seashore of a beautiful land, the wheeling gulls, the stretch of dunes, and the circling procession of clouds over a wind-swept sea. The poetry and dreamy searchings of Copenhagen porcelain have held the mirror to Nature. With outer eye illumined with spiritual vision, the potters have translated the soul of Nature's physical beauty into porcelain. Here is the natural—but there is the vast, unfathomed supernatural. Can it be possible that there are yet other secrets of the magic of the Northlands? Will the inner vision bring forth into the furnace the dreams of the old world deep in the Northern heart, buried these long centuries? Can the potter poet call up the fleets of ghostly ships that set forth from Trondhjem Fjord with King Olaf and Olgafar the mystic boat with neither sail nor helm nor galley oar? All the wealth of dead ages lies as a hidden treasure-house for him who can with wizardry open these portals and bring back the Northern poesie. The Valrafy, or Raven of Battle, loved the swell and the roar of the fierce Northern Main. The ocean sprite frequented the cold waters of the Baltic and flashed, icy bearded, through the rack and cloud of storm. Mermen and mermaidens still plash in the sea-caves where mortals venture not, and to this day in story and tradition they are treasured in the hearts of fisher-folk and those who go down to the sea in ships.

But these are vain imaginings, and to ask more of an art already raised to a plane of evasive and incommunicable inventiveness is to clamour impertinently for the impossible.

TABLE OF MARKS[8]

Used by the leading Painters and Modellers during the Renaissance Period from 1885.

[8] These marks are published by the courtesy of the Royal Copenhagen Porcelain Factory, being supplied from official data, and are strictly copyright.

All these initials or signatures of painters are used in conjunction with the factory mark of the three blue lines.

Various signatures of Arnold Krog, Art Director of the Royal Copenhagen Porcelain Factory since 1885 to the present time.

Examples of the diverse character of the work of Professor Krog permeate the Renaissance period, and include—

Blue fluted service (continuous invention of new forms with elaborate decoration) —

e.g. Dessert Plate (illustrated, p. 249).
Vases with landscapes and bird subjects.

Placques—
Birds, e.g. illustration, p. 203.
Series of heraldic placques, e.g. illustration, p. 243.
Figure Subjects—
Various, including quadrupeds and birds, e.g. Polar bear, Peacock on an urn, etc.
Initials of C. F. Liisberg.
Sometimes the name is signed in full.
Painter of landscapes, quadrupeds, birds, and flowers.
Modeller of animal subjects.
Came to factory in 1885, died in 1909.
For examples of the beauty of the late Hr. Liisberg's work, see illustrations:—
Vase (p. 239).
Placques (pp. 211, 221, 231).

C. Mortensen. Painter of landscape and animal subjects.
Modeller of animals.
1887-1901.

Oluf Jensen. Painter of flower subjects.
1885 to present time.

Aug Hallin. Painter.
1885-1895.

Gotfred Rode. Painter of landscapes and animals.
1895 to present time.
See illustration, p. 217.

Vilh. Th. Fischer. Painter of animal subjects.

1894 to present time.

For illustrations of Hr. Fischer's work, see pp. 211, 217, 239.

V.m. Th Fischer

Stephan Ussing. Painter of flowers and landscapes.

1894 to present time.

St. Ussing

Frk. A. Smidth. Painter of landscapes and flowers.

1885 to present time.

For example of Frk. Smidth's work, see illustration, p. 227.

ASmidth

Frk. M. Høst. Painter of animals and flowers.

MHöst

Frk. Bertha Nathanielsen. Painter of flowers and landscapes.

BERTHA NATHANIELSEN

Frk. Jenny Meyer. Painter of flower subjects.

Jenny Meyer.

Frk. C. Zernichow. Painter of children.

C. ZERNICHOW.

Gerhard Heilmann. Painter of landscapes and animals.

The following mark is found on examples of crystalline glazes of the Renaissance period:—

VE

This is the signature of Hr. V. Engelhardt, the chemist at the royal factory, whose researches have perfected the glazes and won considerable distinction for the factory in European ceramics.

1892 to present time.

For examples of Hr. Engelhardt's work, see illustrations, pp. 293, 297, 299, 303.

The following marks are incised and are of modellers, and are used in conjunction with the factory mark of the three blue lines.

Axel Locher. Modeller of figures.

AXEL LOCHER

E. Nielsen. Modeller of animals.

Christian Thomsen. Modeller of figures and animals.
For examples, see illustrations, pp. 271, 275, 279, 285.

Theodor Madsen. Modeller of animals.

Knud Kyhn. Modeller of animals.

Frk. A. Pedersen. Modeller of animals.

Frk. M. Nielsen. Modeller of birds and fishes.
1903 to present time.

Carl Martin Hansen. Modeller of figures.
1905 to present day.

Gerhard Henning. Modeller and painter of figures.
1909 to present time.

This mark of the factory, with the crown and words "Royal Copenhagen" inscribed in circle are in *green*. The three lines beneath are in blue.

The use of this mark is from the year 1889, on many examples for the English and American markets.

These marks of the crown and the three lines, *in blue*, are used on all copies of the old models of the **overglaze** Müller period. These are found on reproductions of old and rare examples of the early days, made by the factory on traditional lines. The revival of this *overglaze* painting is a new impulse. The artist's initials are added to the crown in colour or gold.

CHAPTER IX

FIGURE SUBJECTS AND GROUPS

RENAISSANCE PERIOD

CHAPTER IX

FIGURE SUBJECTS AND GROUPS

RENAISSANCE PERIOD

Form *versus* colour—The technique of modelling—The sound principles of old Copenhagen porcelain—Underglaze succeeds overglaze colouring—The love of animal life—Peasant types and children.

The highest test to apply to a figure subject in porcelain is that it should be criticized in the biscuit stage. The crudities, the disproportioned ornament or the restless lack of cohesion become at once evident, without the touches of colour added to conceal the poverty of the art.

In our old factories at Plymouth and Bristol in the hard paste and at Bow in the soft paste, owing to an imperfect knowledge of the technique, fire-cracks often appeared in the body of objects intended for ornament. Collectors of experience and mature judgment know exactly what the potters did in these trying circumstances. The scientific examination of the treasures of the china cabinet has revealed many of the potter's tricks. A fire-crack becomes the body of a butterfly gaudily painted in rich colours. This is one instance of the use of colour to conceal the inexactitude of the craftsman. Similarly, in figures it becomes a speculative question as to what their character would turn out to be when they were stripped of the gorgeous costumes with which they are decked. Many a Chelsea figure with rich brocaded surtout, yellow vest, and breeches of amazing colour in scale pattern of peacock hues, would turn out to be a veritable scarecrow if stripped of the glories of pigment. The colour has deceived the eye in regard to form.

This love of colour and disregard of the niceties of form has betrayed many enthusiasts into going into raptures over monstrosities which would not bear the light of day upon them if they were in biscuit state. It is a matter for conjecture how many Staffordshire figures or Toby Jugs, minus pigment, would call for a word of praise judged solely on their modelling and symmetrical beauty.

In Copenhagen, from the early overglaze painted figures of the Müller period to the underglaze decorated figures of the Renaissance style, there is one quality that they have in common. This is especially noticeable in comparing them with work of other factories over an extended period of time. They exhibit with unerring precision the limitations of the potter in regard to the medium in which he works. At no time has the Copenhagen modeller attempted, save in the decadent period when he copied Thorvaldsen's sculpture, to encroach upon the work of the silversmith or the glass-blower. He has been true to the clay whose properties in the fire he knows so well. The technique of modelling in clay follows laws as definite as can well be laid down. It is the same in all crafts where strict observance is paid to the use for which objects are created. The Japanese ivory-carver in his *netsukes*, or ivory fastenings for garments, carves them as nearly oval or round as is possible. It may be a curled-up mouse, or an old man with a barrel, or any other fanciful subject, but the absence of spikes is the sign that the work is old and not modern carving for the European markets, when such objects bristle with points.

Similarly, in figures, for many reasons they should have no jutting arms or over out-thrust ornaments. First because in use they will be broken off. A glance at the damaged specimens on the china shelf will at once show the mistakes of the potter. Rarely at the Copenhagen factory did the modeller fancy for the moment he was a silver-worker and leave a projecting arm. There is one instance in an old figure most noticeable. A seller of *kringler* has an outstretched hand offering his ware for sale, but that is missing in the example the writer examined.

Another reason for the avoidance of undue extension is the technical difficulty of supporting this in the oven during firing. Clay in the oven requires every assistance to keep it from warping or bending over, and to introduce unnecessary difficulties in modelling is to produce bad art. This, coupled with the fact that porcelain shrinks in firing to about six-sevenths of its original size, is sufficient reason for the artistic potter to keep strictly within the limitations of his technique.

The Sound Principles of Old Copenhagen Porcelain.—Throughout the Müller period it will be seen how carefully these axioms were followed. In regard to the styles of decoration, the old school worked in overglaze painting and the Renaissance school employs underglaze painting. They are in complete contrast to one another in the treatment of a subject. The narrow range of underglaze colours in a measure limits the results of the decorator of figures. But it must not be imagined that the overglaze school of painting, by reason of its freer palette, allowed the modelling of the figures to be less than ideal. A reference to the Müller chapter on *Figure Subjects* will show that a great many examples were produced in white or in biscuit, and were thus entirely independent of colour to help out any deficiencies in modelling, if such existed.

An indication of the strong individuality of the figure modelling of the Juliane Marie period, is forthcoming in the fact that the factory to-day is producing some of the coloured figures of that period in white.

Underglaze succeeds Overglaze Colouring.—Concerning the Renaissance figures as a whole, there is a tendency to produce them in white; this bespeaks great strength of modelling, and, varied as they are in character, dealing with different phases of life, they are never insipid. But it may be advanced that the underglaze colours are not extended enough in their range to do justice to some of the costume subjects. It seems to the present writer, and perhaps the criticism is confirmed by a pronounced tendency in that direction by the latest artistic movement in the factory, that many of the modern figures, such as peasant women in costume and the soldier in Hans Andersen's story of the *Tinder Box*, would give more complete results in overglaze painting. This revival of overglaze painting in Copenhagen in figures, and in combination with underglaze work, is a new development which is being curiously watched by connoisseurs and technical experts.

The underglaze colours find complete harmony in the decoration of figures of birds, and are delicate and true to nature in the modelled fish, which have a graceful charm especially their own. They are a perfect medium for placques and vases, depicting the long vaporous clouds stretched across a leaden sky, the silvery blue transparent billows tossing in from the Baltic, or in the foreground streaming wearily over the level grey-yellow sand, flecked with the lilac seashore flowers and tufts of grass on the sand-dunes. The pale sad blues, the delicate greens, the amber, and pink, and dun-grey tones verging into violet which are transmuted in the *grand feu* convey the faint colours, the mist and the sadness, the storm and the rainy air, the dim haze extending over meadow and lake, and the tremulously yellow tones of sunset. The landscape is tinged with that soft melancholy which tones down all harshness and softens all lines. Meditative, somnolent, indecisive, liquid, limpid, and alluring in tender serenity, these characteristics appeal to the soul of the artist as belonging to the dream country of lakes and beech-woods and sand-hills and kaleidoscopic waters. These intangible and wraith-like impressions have been momentarily snatched by the potters and painters at the factory, nor has anything been dropped in the fiery ordeal of the furnace, and they stand in ceramic art as a permanent national record of the homeland of the Dane.

The Love of Animal Life.—There is one point at which the modern figure subjects break new ground. The Renaissance period is rich in its love of the animal kingdom. The wheeling gulls, the wild swans, and geese, and mallards, wading and diving birds, and storks, and owls have been modelled. The wild life of Denmark has provided a new field. This is studied from nature. There is a figure of a turkey, a denizen of the factory grounds, modelled from life. What other factory in the world is there where one may meet, as did the writer, a turkey with her brood being ushered from the garden up a staircase into a pen in one of the studios? The original with her brood may be seen illustrated, p. 337.

FIGURE OF WOMAN AND COW.
Painted in underglaze colours. Modelled by Chr. Thomsen.

      Animals and fish have obtained full recognition in the gallery of figure subjects. The Zoological Gardens in close proximity to the factory has provided the Polar bear and other studies. A notable example of fine modelling is a *Sea Lion*, which is life-like in its faithful representation. The modelled fish, with the liquid glaze suggestive that they have just been captured, are a remarkable feature and are true in every detail—as true as were the botanical specimens on the *Flora Danica* service. They come as decorative objects as surprisingly beautiful in form as are the birds, and their variety captivates the lover of natural form and subdued colour.

      Peasant Types and Children.—The peasant life of the country, the costume, now fast disappearing, and the old-world character, still happily preserved in many districts, were reproduced in the overglaze figures of an earlier period. This love of veracity in costume and environment is a feature which is traditional in the factory; it therefore comes as no surprise to find that peasant types are produced with underglaze treatment in colours. The only example of an animal in the overglaze Müller period is the *Woman milking a Cow*, and a similar subject of a Milkmaid and Cow may be seen treated in modern manner in underglaze style, with delicate suggestion of colour in the pale grey dress, delicate blue shawl, and kerchief with infinitesimal spots. The cow is white save for one or two splashes of light brown.

If Cupids be child-life, then the old style offers scores of examples, but the modern child has been denuded of his wings and is employed in other occupations than twining wreaths of roses around lovers. The usual children of the china shelf are armed with baskets and posies, and are Cupid-like in their character. But in the Renaissance figures of Copenhagen children the spirit of childhood is present. The simple peasant *Child* (illustrated, p. 279), with burden of bottle and basket, is as true to life as the faithful record of an old Dutch master. It is, possibly without meaning to be, symbolic of the life of toil of the peasant. It is a tale the clay tells of the busy life of the fields. Even a tiny child has to bear her share of the long day's work. It is just that sad touch of reflection which illuminates great works of art, and it is here present. A figure such as this is worth, as a work of art, fifty meaningless Rockingham *Flower Boys* or Chelsea manikins in grotesque costume.

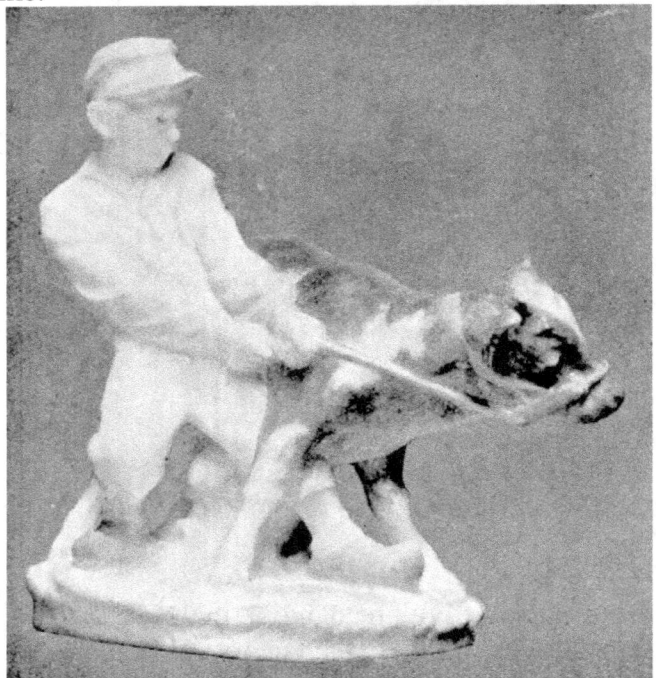

FIGURE OF BOY AND CALF.
Painted in underglaze colours. Modelled by Chr. Thomsen.

The *Old Woman*, modelled by the same artist, with bonnet and shawl with fringe, represents a type now belonging to days rapidly passing. The character of an obsolescent type has been caught with exceptional cleverness. There is another figure of an old woman less robust, and indicating less lovable qualities, with Bible in hand, and, if the truth be told, a somewhat crafty look. Such types as these will be recognized by those who know Denmark well; they are racy of the soil, and represent the acute perception of the modern potters in seizing disappearing types. Such crystallized character forms a permanent and very valuable record of the remoter side of country life, and is instinct with a truer feeling of art than whole galleries representing impossible porcelain cavaliers and ladies in costume the like of which no man has ever seen.

In dealing with the underglaze ware from its first application to utilitarian services to its subtle use in placques and vases with *grand-feu* colours, and finally in figure subjects and groups, it will be seen, both in regard to mastery of technique and artistic evolution, the natural order of development is that given in Chapter II in examining the stages of overglaze painting and modelling. At that period the order proceeds on lines of its own, and the usual stages of progression were influenced by the fact that in the early days of the factory Luplau, the first modelling-master, brought his experience to bear on the work, and figure subjects of a high order were attempted almost from the beginning. Here, in the Renaissance period, by slower evolution and particularly sure processes, the modelling of figures has arrived at a state of undoubted excellence. Apart from the first early inspiration when things Japanese broke upon Europe with overwhelming force, the Copenhagen artists have obtained their inspiration from within. They have followed the instincts of their own race, and they have developed on lines essentially their own, both in form, in colour, and in technique.

The Europe of sixty years ago was sated with meaningless formalities. Tired with the repetition of the scanty stock of Greek ornaments, and in search of novelty, it is only natural that men should turn their eyes to the only living schools of decorative art then in existence. In India, China, and Japan was found the freshness that design needed. When Müller was producing his masterpieces in clay, Wedgwood was transplanting Greek gods and goddesses into Staffordshire, and Chippendale was fashioning his fretwork angles to tables and chairs, taken direct from China. Between those days and the present is the great wave of classicism which dug out Etruscan vases and remodelled them, brought the Latin chair into the early nineteenth-century drawing-room, and with stilted affectation of simplicity drove elegance and comfort far afield.

PEASANT FIGURES.
Painted in underglaze colours. Modelled by Chr. Thomsen.

Of all Oriental schools it is thus natural that the Japanese, with the unexpected and unsymmetrical treatment of design, should appeal most at such a time. The true and fine feeling of the Japanese for birds and beasts, for the flower world and for landscape in its larger features, is shown in all their design, from the small ivory carvings to the lacquer work or the colour prints of Katsuchika Hokusai. The West has learned much from the East in the nineteenth century. Whistler's Nocturnes and Aubrey Beardsley's pen drawings catch their germ of novelty from sources other than European.

But "East is East and West is West," and Copenhagen underglaze decoration has produced the tones of the Northern world. Of all curious happenings, it is singular to record that to-day the Japanese ceramic artists are fashioning their work in the same subdued tones, and producing similar subjects in figures, to the little band of ceramic workers in Denmark. In the history of the manufacture of porcelain this is not exactly a new thing. In England we have Worcester copying Chinese examples and inventing a pseudo mark, and the Bow and Lowestoft factories copying Worcester's copy of Chinese originals. Meissen and Sèvres have both suffered heavily from votaries who have loved the originals so well that they could not forbear from imitating them. In England, at Worcester and at Coalport, the copyists excelled in their love for the Sèvres and Meissen originals by putting the marks of those factories on their productions.

It is a remarkable fact that Denmark, with no coal and with no minerals, and with no quartz and no china clay, should stand to-day as the leading porcelain factory in Europe. In the admirable article on *Ceramics* in the new edition of the *Encyclopædia Britannica* (1911) this verdict stands: "The most admirable result of this revived interest in Japanese art was, however, developed at the Royal Copenhagen works, the productions of which are not only famous all over the world, but have set a new style in porcelain decorations which is being followed at most of the Continental factories." In connection with figure subjects the same critic recognizes their precious qualities. "The Royal Copenhagen works have also produced a profusion of skilfully modelled animals, birds, and fishes, either in pure white or tinted after nature with the same underglaze colours. Other European factories have adopted the modern Copenhagen style of decoration."

Something should be said in passing of the domestic influence of the Royal Copenhagen Factory upon the art of Denmark. Like a sturdy oak-tree, the old factory has continued in its steady growth from the days of Queen Juliane Marie. It has weathered many storms, and now proudly rears its head as a beloved landmark. Its influence on generations of artists has been deep and lasting. It has scattered its *largesse*, and its sheltering branches have lent their protecting shade to many grateful pilgrims. In common with many another great factory, it has added new impulses to the centre of its origin. Like the acorn dropping from the parent tree, productive of flourishing young oaks, so has it been with the royal factory. It is pleasurable to be able to record here the successes of a Copenhagen porcelain factory conducted by Messrs. Bing and Gröndahl. Their art is fresh and winning, their painters have caught the touch of the royal factory, and their modellers have found inspiration in the work marked with the three blue lines. The Bing and Gröndahl ware is marked with the initials B & G. It was originated in the year 1853, and has been marked with a successful career. Many of its productions are to be found in museums side by side with work of the royal factory. There is a spirit of friendly rivalry between the ancestor and the youthful scion. This is only natural. But the old oak and the young tree will still continue to flourish side by side, and the old oak will always be the monarch of the forest, even a hundred years hence, when painstaking collectors wrangle as to dates and marks and weigh the B & G with the three blue lines, and find, as undoubtedly they will, beauty and poetry reminiscent of the Danish art.

Many of the early figure subjects of the Renaissance period were of surprising originality, and in some cases only one example was made. The collectors who were fortunate enough to secure these examples have since realized how happy was their choice. There is one figure of a *Black Cat*, exhibited at the Paris Exhibition, 1900, which has never been repeated in black, owing to the great difficulty experienced in manipulating the glaze and the hazardous nature of the experiment. White cats have been modelled in similar fashion, but there is only one black Copenhagen cat, and naturally such a rare piece is exceedingly valuable.

Among some of the later productions in figures are some finely modelled subjects taken from Hans Christian Andersen's *Stories*. Who does not remember the *Tinder Box*, that tale of enchantment where the soldier, coming home from the wars, marching along the road with knapsack on back, meets a witch who induces him to descend into the great cavern and procure the magic tinder box. A dainty little group in white represents the *Soldier and the Witch*. We know of his sudden rise to fortune, armed with a talisman as potent as Aladdin's Lamp. The sleeping princess imprisoned in a copper castle is brought to him by the faithful canine genii of the tinder box. How he narrowly escaped the gallows and finally took the princess as his bride is one of our own nursery stories, and there is a Copenhagen figure group showing the soldier with his arm around the princess in soldierly and lover-like fashion.

GROUP IN WHITE PORCELAIN.
The Princess and the Swineherd.
(From Hans Christian Andersen's *Stories*.)
Modelled by Chr. Thomsen.

The story of the *Swineherd* provides another subject, and what grace and elegance and beauty are in the lines, and delicacy in the sentiment. It is an idyll in porcelain. Away with pierrots and mimes, the fevered extravagances of imagination run riot in bizarre form and garish colour! Such a group as this should have a niche to itself in the china cabinet. It is superlatively chaste and reticent, daintily conceived and faultless in technique. The story is of the prince who became swineherd to the father of the weary princess. His taste for music took a mechanical turn in the whimsical invention of a pot that played tunes when it boiled, and, among other like toys, a rattle that would play waltzes and polkas. His hobby gained the fancy of the princess, who had to buy them with kisses. The porcelain represents the completion of the fairy-tale bargain. Alas! there is no happy ending, for the kissing became so fast and furious that the swineherd threw off his disguise, became prince on a sudden, and departed home to his kingdom, in disgust with a princess who could look with disdain on his presents of a rose and a nightingale because they were only natural, and set her affections on the trivialities of a swineherd.

Among the figures calling for regard in the highest sense, that of the *Peacock* standing on an urn, modelled by Arnold Krog, is of surprising grace and symmetry. Its modelling is at once true to nature and true to the requirements of the potter's art. A model on a lower plane would have placed the peacock on a base or tree-stump and utilized this as a support, and no figure would be complete without the gorgeous colouring of the tail. This is exactly what happens in a Derby figure of a Peacock (at the Victoria and Albert Museum). On a rococo base covered with a wealth of coloured flowers, a peacock stands in brilliant natural colouring. But in the Copenhagen figure the drooping tail is support enough in the kiln, and the natural pose of the bird, proud and erect, conveys dignity and beauty of form. The treatment at Copenhagen is exactly the opposite to the old school of ceramic artists. Here it is beauty of form first and colour in reticent subjection as an adjunct, and the results are undeniably superlative.

CHAPTER X

CRYSTALLINE GLAZES

CHAPTER X

CRYSTALLINE GLAZES

Flambé or transmutation glazes of the Chinese potters—The Royal Copenhagen Factory produces the first specimen of crystallized glaze in 1886—Blue crackled glaze produced with design under control.

During the last decade of the nineteenth century the Western potter came under the spell of the modern chemist. Scientific study applied to the body and glaze and vitrifaction of the materials composing porcelain and faience, together with a closer study of the exact conditions of temperatures in the kilns, resulted in the discovery of certain well-defined decorative qualities in connection with glazes which, after considerable experiment, offered practically a new field for colour-work of a very beautiful nature.

In the *flambé* or transmutation glazes for which the Chinese potters were renowned, the effects of variegated or splashed colour are due to the capricious action of the fire on the glazes during the firing process. The single-coloured glazes of the Chinese applied to vases and other objects have been much prized by Europeans. The tints are very numerous, sea-green or celadon, yellow, red, blue, purple, brown, black, and other tones. These include the celebrated *sang-de-bœuf* colour of French collectors, so highly prized in China. It is thought probable that many of these single-colour glazes have been applied at a somewhat lower temperature, termed by the French *demi-grand feu*.

The mottled classes owe their appearance less to the difference in the colouring matter than to the manner in which it is applied. They are termed in French *flambé*, and there is no doubt that they were originally accidentally produced. According to the letters of a Jesuit missionary, Père d'Entrecolles, written in the early years of the eighteenth century, such vases were called *Yao pien* or *transmutation* vases. Such types, with turquoise colour passing into green, green melting into purple, and amber fading into grey, are suggestive of the permutation of colour harmonies which these transmutation glazes undergo in the furnace.

Beside the *flambé* glazes there are crackled glazes of turquoise-blue, apple-green, or of greyish white. This crackle porcelain is now artificially produced, but it doubtless owes its origin to accident and caprice of firing.

POLAR BEARS ON AN ICE FLOE.
Modelled by C. E. Bonnesen. Crystalline glaze by V. Engelhardt.

In *flambé* glazes an English potter, Mr. Bernard Moore, of Longton, has succeeded in producing *sang-de-bœuf* colour with delightful gradations of tone; unhappily, some of these pieces were destroyed by fire at the Brussels Exhibition in 1910.

Copenhagen produces the First Crystalline Glaze.—At the Copenhagen factory *grand-feu* coloured glazes have been developed in a remarkable manner. The crystal glaze, the serpent-skin, the tiger-eye, and crackled glaze, as well as many other varieties, show effects which hitherto have been unknown in porcelain, and have won the admiration of all connoisseurs. The inception of the crystalline glaze was due to Hr. Clement, the chemist at the Royal Copenhagen Factory, and it was owing to the indefatigable energy and experiments of Hr. Clement that, in 1886, the first piece of porcelain with crystalline glaze achieved a record for the Copenhagen laboratory and studio. Since that day other European potters have succeeded in producing crystalline glazed ware of exceptional beauty.

We illustrate a fine specimen of the early crystalline glaze of Copenhagen now preserved at the Museum of the National Porcelain Manufactory at Sèvres. It represents a frog on a leaf. "We should like specially to point out," says M. Edouard Garnier, the Director of the Museum at Sèvres, writing in 1894, "a large water-lily leaf on which a frog is imbedded in a thin layer of ice, which it has just succeeded in breaking. We have never seen a more striking example of what may be attained by a purely scientific process applied to art decoration, and we cannot repress the wish that this example may be followed by our modern ceramists." This is one of Arnold Krog's fine conceptions.

This specimen of the work of the Copenhagen chemist, Hr. V. Engelhardt, in crystallized glaze, has been followed by many notable achievements on his part. In 1902 there was a figure of a *Polar Bear* lapping water, modelled by Arnold Krog and produced in crystalline glaze by Hr. Engelhardt. This, of which only thirty pieces were made, was executed for an artistic club in Paris. Another fine subject is that representing two Polar Bears on the ice, one mounted on a frozen pinnacle. The whole is a skilful piece of modelling by C. E. Bonnesen, and crystalline glazing by Hr. V. Engelhardt.

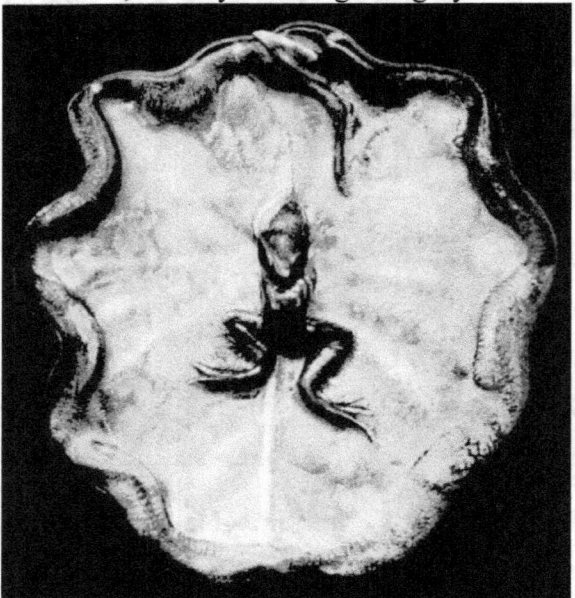

**FROG IMBEDDED IN ICE ON A WATER-LILY LEAF.
Modelled by Arnold Krog. Crystalline glaze by V. Engelhardt.
Period 1891-1895.
(*At Sèvres Museum.*)]**

VASES.
Designed by Arnold Krog. Crystalline glaze by V. Engelhardt.

New shapes are continually being invented, and a long chain of experiments in the laboratory has resulted in the production of some very remarkable examples of colouring which are always welcome to collectors, who are quick to realize that no two examples can ever be the same. All colours can be handled in this manner. The range is a wide one, and the surprising gradations of tone have a charm undoubtedly their own, and not unworthy to be regarded as representative of some of the most wonderful creations of the modern potter. The metallic oxides in the hands of the twentieth-century chemist become possessed of magical properties and are transformed into tender harmonies vibrating with exquisite tones. Yellows, and blues, and browns merge into mauve or grey, in delightful tenderness, and black and white are included in the colour schemes of which this style is now capable.

Blue Crackled Glaze.—In regard to crackled glazes there is evidence that they are coming more under the governance of the chemist. There is a beautiful deep blue variety produced at Copenhagen, with a network of crackle graduated to a nicety, now swelling, when on the belly of the beaker or vase, and now contracting into minute meshes when on the slender neck. This is completely under mechanical control. As yet blue is the only colour produced in this style.

At the Brussels Exhibition, 1910, the Sèvres factory exhibited some large vases with crystalline glaze evidently under the complete mastery of the potter and chemist. These vases were of a very fine character, and the suggestion arises that at no far distant date the glazes now termed "transmutation" or adventitious will be completely mastered by the latest developments of modern science as applied to pottery, and thus "transmutation" will be a word of the past.

The technique of Copenhagen differs from that of Sèvres or of Berlin. In these latter cases the crystals appear like spots on the surface, whereas in Copenhagen ware the crystals have a more subtle and intimate incorporation with the glaze. They never stand on the surface, and often, as in the mellow brown glaze, they lie beneath and glow in reflected light.

A series of effects in broken colour, delicate in marking and veined and mottled in most pleasing character, is being attempted in vases. We illustrate several types in whole and partial crystallization, which lose considerably by appearing as black-and-white illustrations. Such vases are conspicuous for their revelry in colour, not the hard, dense, opaque colours of the old Chinese single glazes, but the limpid, vibrating, restless subtleties of Nature's own play of pulsating colours in changeful mood—the dazzling and fairy-like opalescence of the frost and the deep blue of the ice cave, or the pale amber sand-dunes imperceptibly fading into a translucent green stretch of waters, with the vaporous haze of a violet sky. In the white heat of the modern furnace the flowers of a prehistoric day, which have lain buried in the coal seams of an alien land, transmute the dull clay and the mineral glaze under the hand of the modern magician into colour nocturnes.

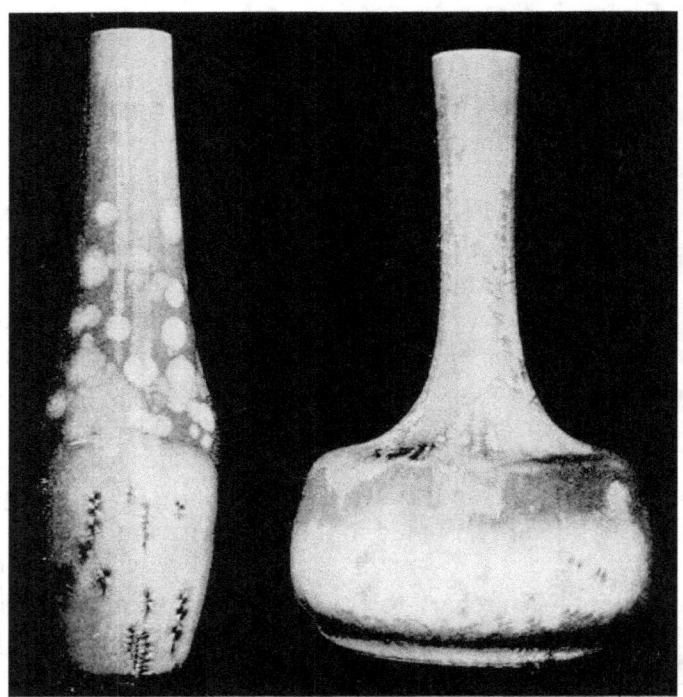

VASES.
With Crystalline glazes by V. Engelhardt.

COPENHAGEN ART FAIENCE.
Dish, with tropical bird, decorated in rich colours. Designed by Christian Joachim.

CHAPTER XI

COPENHAGEN ART FAIENCE

The inception of a new technique—The slow growth of a new art—The old masters of majolica—The great promise of a new school—The rich output of colour and inventive form.

The student of ceramic art well knows that porcelain and earthenware, although as poles asunder in their technique, do oftentimes touch one another in apparent affinity. For instance, what is more earthen than the brown crumbling body of the Dutch delft ware? It is a poor relation of porcelain. But the Dutch potter had in mind the great prototypes of the East. His dishes and his jars were an attempt to copy blue-and-white Kang-He porcelain. He covered his brown body with a white enamel and painted his tulips and his Batavian-Chinese designs to imitate the Dutch East India Company's examples he had before him. He created a new art, but he started as a copyist. Beautiful as is Delft, it is really only a simulation in earthenware of blue-and-white porcelain. Similarly in regard to English earthenware, with the noteworthy exceptions of a few types essentially true to the technique of earthenware, it is singular how peculiarly obtuse the Staffordshire potters have been to the limitations of earthenware. They have assiduously attempted to bring it into line with porcelain in its decoration and its appearance. The line of demarcation between earthenware and porcelain has become in England very indefinite, owing to the fact that true porcelain is not manufactured in this country. In consequence, the artificial composition of the body of English porcelain, where calcined bones form an addition to the Chinese formula of true porcelain, has brought it into closer relationship with earthenware than is the case in any other European porcelain. "Semi-porcelain," a term in English ceramics, is not to be found elsewhere. It is still a moot-point whether to classify Wedgwood's jasper ware as earthenware or porcelain. "Ironstone china," a hardware introduced by Mason in 1830 and copied by other potters, is earthenware, and the instances could be multiplied of confusion in nomenclature. But where, as on the Continent, only hard paste that is true porcelain in the Chinese manner is produced, save at Sèvres, the distinction between this and earthenware is most clearly defined.

COPENHAGEN ART FAIENCE.
Placque, with parrot, decorated in rich colours by Christian Joachim.

At Copenhagen, therefore, the manufacture of faience at a porcelain factory was a leap into the unknown. Not only were different kilns to be employed, but a different technique and especial conditions governed the manufacture. The theories which had been skilfully put into practice and the ideals which had been reached in the art of porcelain were alien to the new departure in the field of faience. To have welded together the two arts and the two techniques would have ruined the enterprise at its commencement. The two streams were allowed to run apart, and the result is an artistic achievement no less noteworthy than the Renaissance of the Royal Copenhagen porcelain. The mantle of Philip Schou has descended on his son-in-law, Frederik Dalgas, who has ably continued the traditions of his predecessor in the management of this national enterprise. The inception and development of this art faience of Copenhagen is due to Mr. Frederik Dalgas, who brought a keen and virile intuition into this new field of ceramic adventure. Whereas in the porcelain there is delicate artistry and finesse, in the faience there is breadth and vivacity of colour schemes. Never do the twain touch each other in kinship. The faience is not a poor kinsman of the porcelain. It is a new creation, a fresh and forceful note in ceramic art. It has a relationship with bygone majolica of another land. It is a transplantation of a southern stock into a northern clime. One is reminded of those labels at Kew Gardens indicating that certain rare trees from sunnier lands have been acclimatized and have become beauty spots in a far country.

The Slow Growth of a New Art.—It is always interesting to the student to examine specimens belonging to the experimental stage of an art. It is here that the potter struggling with his new technique betrays in his *motifs* suggestions as to its origin. There are very few wares in ceramic art that stand out as supremely original. In some way or another they bear relationship to earlier potters' work, as a rule. Whole schools of artistic potters have been avowedly copyist. This is a truism in regard to European ceramic art as a whole: it is admittedly derivative from Oriental prototypes. But in regard to various branches of pottery apart from porcelain, there is little doubt that it has a long lineage. It is therefore possible to compare the stages of evolution of faience in the Western countries and to realize that since Greek and Roman and Etruscan days man was a progressive potter, though even in this field derivative technique came from east of Suez. The earliest examples of the Copenhagen faience suggest that the old Italian majolica models had lingered in the memory of the potters making their essay into a new domain. Those who have carefully watched the slow but sure growth of this art faience of Copenhagen will have come to realize how surely the potter has put his foot on a new plane and established something that is characteristic and original. He has by a gradual process year by year added new forms, created dishes and beakers of sound design, and perfected the decorations in colour till they have reached something which is gay without being garish and exuberant in rich colouring without being other than surprisingly harmonious. One wonders how the Oriental rug-weaver can place his blues and his reds seemingly so disastrous to tone effect. But there they are, and, either by strong contrast or perfect harmony, the results are artistically true. It is the same question one asks of the colour effects in the Copenhagen art faience. They are perfectly luscious and strikingly original. No one else has employed these combinations of pigments, nor their wide range of colours. They appear to have been produced by magic. But to any one with a working knowledge of a great factory will come the reflection that the apparent magic is the wizardry of genius, and genius has been defined as the infinite capacity for taking pains. The strenuous work, the long vigils, the indefatigable and indomitable determination to accomplish the mastery of the technique is here evident. It is the strong and fruitful harvest of a slow growth carefully tended in an especially artistic environment by trained minds.

COPENHAGEN ART FAIENCE.
Vase, decorated with sprays of flowers in rich colours.

The Old Masters of Majolica.—The Italian school with its glazed ware of polychrome decorative effects, Faenza, Caffaggiolo, Urbino, Pesarro, and later its lustre (notably the ruby ware of Gubbio), was partially derivative from Persian and from Hispano-Moresque prototypes. Figure subjects form an important feature. Groups in contemporary costume, portraits, and religious or allegorical subjects, as well as heraldic devices, occupy the centre of the dish. But the border is a framework which is richly decorated with brilliant and varied colours. The designs are conceived in the best vein of sixteenth-century fecundity of invention. Elaborate floriate ornament is in combination with satyrs and grotesque masks, or cupids, or birds, or sea monsters. It suggests the sprightly grace which enlivens the tail-pieces engraved in contemporary Italian books. Design, till it ran riot later, was exuberant, and there seemed no end to the outburst of originality and imagination.

It is to these old masters, particularly of the Italian period from about 1480 to about 1580, that one turns for great ideas and perfect execution. Before the latter date signs were evident that the art was declining: already the secret of the Gubbio ruby lustre had been lost.

The earlier Persian pottery and the Rhodian ware, produced as far afield as Damascus and Ispahan, had disseminated the wondrous technique of the East. The Hispano-Moresque ware of Malaga and Valencia, a century earlier than the greatest period of the Italian school, gradually lost its Moorish character with arabesque design and pseudo-Arabic characters, till, in the late sixteenth century, designs in contemporary

Spanish costume and broad floriate borders found favour. The copper lustre was, however, still a feature.

COPENHAGEN ART FAIENCE.
Vase with hexagonal top and base, richly decorated with flowers and arabesque ornament, by Christian Joachim.

It is obvious, therefore, that the old masters are the fount from which so much has been derived. Nevers, Rouen, and Moustiers caught the colour-schemes of Persia and Italy, and each in turn made them her own. In studying the finest work of the old masters of faience we see that the technique is something very different from what Staffordshire has made it. John Dwight in the seventeenth, and Thomas Whieldon in the eighteenth century both worked on sound lines. It is not high art to attempt to make faience simulate porcelain, any more than it is when wall paper pretends to be marble, or leather, or tapestry. Porcelain shows as much of its white body and sparkling glaze as is possible. It depends, as does an etching, on its uncovered background for its luminous effects and its atmosphere. Faience is like an oil painting: it demands that the whole surface be covered. It has a yellow, or brown, or green, or lilac ground. The decoration, in contradistinction to porcelain, is broad and strong. There are no finicking "Chantilly sprigs" in faience. Bold, virile, and striking must be the notes that dominate faience, but withal—and herein lies the supremest difficulty—it must be naïve and simple. It must not suggest the palace, and certainly not the boudoir. It must bespeak the open air. It is the perennial herbaceous border in ceramic art, and not the hot-house or the conservatory.

The Great Promise of a New School.—Lovers of Copenhagen ware and connoisseurs who were aware of the possibilities of faience produced under rightly understood principles have not been disappointed in the art faience which Mr. Christian

Joachim has made his own under a group of trained artist potters. His is the guerdon of praise, and the laurel wreath should be placed on his head for his services to the art of his native country. He has happily received the support of a farseeing directorate. His life record will stand as a great triumph for the Copenhagen art faience. What Arnold Krog has done in porcelain, Christian Joachim has done in faience. With a fine appreciation of the limitations of his technique, and with a bold imagination as to further possibilities in modern conditions, he has sent forth his pottery with a message of gaiety and youth. No man is a prophet in his own country. But in Europe and in America Christian Joachim's work has become noteworthy. Danes the world over buy it because it is Danish. We English and other strangers buy it because it is beautiful art.

COPENHAGEN ART FAIENCE.
       Figures. *A Midsummer Night's Dream.* Modelled by R. Harboe.
       Bottom the Weaver.
Fairy.
Philostrate, Master of the Revels.

      In an examination of the art tendencies of the new school, it would appear that in the attempt to be surprisingly original there is the wilful abandonment of anything suggestive of Persian, or Rhodian, or Moorish, or Italian ideals. The *motifs* are especially modern, and the schemes of colour are skilfully handled in a novel manner, and owing to scientific development the potter's palette is more extensive than heretofore. The promise has already been fulfilled, and connoisseurs await later developments with no little curiosity.

      The Rich Output of Colour and Inventive Form.—The illustrations to this chapter lack colour, and therefore they cannot do justice to what is one of the most important features in the new art faience. Among the pigments that are used are the following, no incomplete range in comparison with what has gone before in this ceramic field. The Dutch found blue the least refractory of colours, and adhered largely to its use till later they employed yellow. Rouen employed yellow and red and green. But Copenhagen has a palette consisting of cream, yellow, green, blue, red, lilac, and a warm plum colour or purple. This latter colour, the product of scientific modernity, is wielded with a sure hand by Christian Joachim and his school of artists. It is in such examples as the dish and the placque with tropical birds (illustrated, pp. 307, 311) that the rich colour effects procurable are seen at their best. In the placque extreme simplicity and artlessness of design is exhibited in the floral border. In the dish the border is luxuriant with colour, although broad in treatment. Such examples are extremely decorative, and exhibit this branch of ceramic art on a high level. They attain their excellence by methods of their own. They cannot be confounded with the productions of any other factory, either older or contemporary. Their originality is a factor not to be eliminated in adjudging them.

In vases and other vessels demanding attention to form there is apparent the striving, natural in all potters, for unique forms. A fine vase with rich floral decoration (illustrated, p. 315) follows the early Italian drug pot. Another breaks new ground, and its square hexagonal surfaces require a touch of geometric ornament, rarely found in Copenhagen faience (illustrated, p. 319). Punch-bowls with covers, having as a knob a full-sized lemon in natural colours, are novel and utilitarian. The modelling of Mr. Harboe and of Mr. Slott-Möller is deserving of recognition. *A Midsummer Night's Dream* was performed some years ago in the open air in a glade in the Deerhavn, near Copenhagen, before some thousands of people. It is natural, therefore, to find little faience figures of Bottom the Weaver, of Flute the Bellows-mender, and of Philostrate the Master of the Revels, of Puck, of Oberon and of Titania, and of delightful fairies. These are not conjured up from the German translation by Schlegel of Shakespeare's plays, but from Shakespeare's own imaginings, minus the addition of the heavy hand of German *Kultur*. We do not remember that Staffordshire has attempted to reproduce Shakespearean characters in clay, though at one time, after Wedgwood, Jupiter and Venus and other alien gods and goddesses were found on every cottager's mantelshelf. The Copenhagen figures of *Clown*, *Columbine*, and *Harlequin* are pleasing in their graceful simplicity (illustrated, p. 327).

COPENHAGEN ART FAIENCE.
Figures—Clown, Columbine, and Harlequin—by Christian Joachim.

Boxes—*bonbonnières* as the French term them—are produced in great variety. We reproduce two, broadly decorated and having covers with original design of bird and wood sprite. This latter follows the true canons of plastic art. He is as rotund, with no breakable projections, as a Japanese ivory button *netsuke*. With them is illustrated a vase Persian in character, but with modern colour effects. All this is excellent, but one asks for more. In wishing the new school of the North *bon voyage*, we may be allowed to express a hope that it will continue its outburst of resplendent colour and perpetuate its virile design, that it may worthily vie with the great masters of faience in the South and in the East. In regard to personal inclinations, the writer would like to see sometimes embodied in the decorative borders of placques and vases the interlaced work of Runic design, symbolic of the Norse mystery and magic. If the Italian saints find place on the *tazzas* of Faenza, surely Thor and Wodin, who gave their names to two days of the week, and other heroes of Northern mythology, should be embodied in this Copenhagen gallery. The triumphs of the Vikings and their sagas quicken the imagination. Of heroes of later date, one could wish to see Cnut at the English seashore, or the rugged portrait of old Christian IV.

It may be that these vain cravings for pages from the past run not attune to the dreams of the master potter with an eye to the future; possibly decorative technique forbids—but here are the stray lines of a foreign spectator in kindly spirit.

The ware is marked in green with an italic *A* to signify its origin from the parent Aluminia factory as early as 1863, and to this are added the three lines so well known as a Royal Copenhagen Porcelain mark.

COPENHAGEN ART FAIENCE.
Vase and Boxes with lids surmounted by wood sprite and by bird, richly decorated in colours. By H. Slott-Möller and Christian Joachim.

CHAPTER XII

THE FACTORY TO-DAY

Its situation and surroundings—Facilities for the study of plant, flower, and animal life—Modern equipment in machinery and in hygienic improvements—The absence of lead poisoning—New impulses.

In the word *factory* there is nothing suggestive of poetry. In England it represents the Frankenstein who has slain many cottage industries. In connection with our own potteries there are the Five Towns, merged into one, with a quarter of a million of inhabitants. They stand for organized science and applied manufacture. Their architecture is an architecture of chimney-shafts and kilns, black with smoke. It is a prosperous district, crammed with the workers in a gigantic industry. There are visions of murky canals and great hills of accumulated rubble of the mines, coal and copper and iron, dug from the bowels of the earth and blotting out the skyline.

There are crowded byways filled with hurrying operatives, men and women and girls. The beauty of the rich, green, undulating lands of Staffordshire has been effaced by this delving of human moles. It is as though some ruthless giant had made sport of the hills and worked havoc on a smiling plain. But modern life demands sacrifices, and chinaware must be made to send to the four corners of the earth—this is the great White Country.

In Denmark things are managed differently. It comes as a welcome surprise to the English visitor, educated to other scenes, to find the Royal Porcelain Factory set in a pleasant suburb of the city near the old gardens of the Palace of Frederiksberg. One cannot have an omelette without breaking eggs: the factory chimneys are there, the green-hedged paths are surely a snare leading up to another such prison-house as are all factories the world over. Here are the heaps of quartz, and we catch the hum of the machinery. The workers are in the hive; some unkind sprite has snatched them from the pleasant ways of a delightful city set by the sea and immured them for their sins in this fortress of stone.

COURTYARD OF ROYAL COPENHAGEN FACTORY.
Showing turkey and brood.

It suggests the story of Böttger and his workmen imprisoned by reason of the secrets they held. Surely these workmen and artists who know the secret of the Copenhagen ware will not be allowed to escape. It is too precious a thing to Denmark that its secrets be divulged. But the reply comes suddenly when the doors are opened and the secret, that is no secret, is disclosed. These men and women are Danes, and proud of their art and filled with the love of their Copenhagen porcelain. They come and go as they will. Like bees they roam over the flowers and the gems of nature, and they return home to the hive because they love their art. That which their hand findeth to do, they do with all their might.

Facility for Study of Animal and Plant Life.—There is sunshine here in this Northern pottery. The courtyard shows a scene no other factory in the world can offer; it is bewildering to a student of potteries: a turkey with her brood proudly dominates the scene. We have with the camera caught this as a record. It is as suggestive as it is remarkable that the artists have carried their love for fidelity so far that flowers and animals and birds find themselves in suitable environment at this strange enchanted factory.

Animal life is dear to the potters here. There are over three hundred moulds of different types—wading and diving wild fowl from the remoter "haunts of coot and hern"; sea-gulls, never absent from the harbour and canals spanned by bridges over which trams pass; bears and seals, the originals of which are to be found at the Zoological Gardens close by; and if the Phœnix—that fabulous bird which lives for five hundred years, making its nest of spices and burning itself to ashes, coming forth with renewed life for another five hundred years—could be captured, it would find a place in the aviary of the factory which, Phœnix-like, has arisen with youth and vigour.

The Absence of Lead Poisoning.—In place of the white-faced factory workers, we find at the Copenhagen factory a healthy band of workmen, artisans, and artists, employed in conditions that are a credit to all concerned. The usual drudgery of a pottery is eliminated as much as possible in this factory. The latest modern appliances to ventilate the dust-laden air are in use. *There are no cases of lead-poisoning, because lead* *is not used in the factory either in pigments or in glazes.* A dining-hall and dressing-rooms have been erected for the workmen. The factory provides its own electricity and mechanical power; it is heated throughout by hot water, and has a complete system of vacuum and pressure mains.

The lady artists work in almost ideal conditions. They are installed in studios filled with flowers and plants, and in no other factory are the artistic conditions so favourable to the study of plant and animal life. The photographs we reproduce are taken of the normal surroundings of everyday work.

INTERIOR OF ROYAL COPENHAGEN PORCELAIN FACTORY.
Showing studios of lady artists.

The writer has indelible memory pictures of the workmen at the machinery, or in the open air turning over the quartz where it lies in heaps "weathering," exposed to the sun and the frost, of slowly grinding stones revolving in a vat mixing and amalgamating the raw materials, in preparing them for the next stage of handling, revealing the slow and patient processes of the potter's art. There is something hazardous in manipulating the raw materials, crushing them into powder, and bringing them together in the correct proportions for the body. It is here that the long traditions of the factory, the well-guarded secrets in the mixing, and the skilful instinct in conjunction with scientific exactitude, come into full operation. The result is evident in the smooth, white, pearly body and the transparent liquid glaze, so technically perfect and so much admired by other potters.

One recalls an anxious and expectant group at the ovens when a firing is being removed after the ovens have cooled down from the intense heat of the *grand feu*, a temperature never attempted by the manufacturers of soft-paste porcelain in this country.

The laboratory holds mysteries of its own. It is an inner sanctum to which few penetrate. These little human touches indicate that there is a romance in manufacture as well as in more stirring scenes to the accompaniment of the roll of the drum or the rousing bugle-call. The potter's art is rich in associations which render the arts of peace as alluring in story as the arts of war. Many victories have been won in silence, but no less triumphant for that, and these represent man's conquest of earth and the white-hot flame of the furnace, whereby he transmutes the rocks from the quarry and the mountain-side into crystal vases reflecting those same mountains, and streams, and placid lakes, and clouds in stately procession. This is the art of the magician, and modern science has added one more laurel wreath to her victories over the elements.

The interior of a great factory where art is in the making has many exciting moments. The cruel fire is no respecter of persons. After the various steps have been taken, the grinding, the mixing, the moulding into form, the firing in biscuit, the painting, and the subsequent glazing, the creation comes out of the oven as a finished work of art. At any one of these stages a slip may mean disaster. Each successive process gains in difficulty. It is a tragic instant when the last hour is reached. After the oven has cooled the news goes round that a firing is being taken from the kiln. A knot of artists gathers round as each piece comes out. Some call for admiration; there is a hush of joyful surprise when a completed masterpiece comes forth perfect. Alas! too often some delightful dream with its tender colours has twisted out of shape in the intense heat. A graceful form has coalesced with a neighbouring vase. They stand as failures, and the workman with swift, relentless hand gives them a tap with a hammer, and they become shards. The poet-painter's dream has ended in nothingness.

New Impulses.—In regard to the future there are golden hopes and happy anticipations. The past has been glorious, the present is triumphant. A true and living school of design amid sound artistic environment has its band of artist-potters, trained under happy auspices, whose aims are set steadfastly on art that is nothing unless it be national—these are the children of to-morrow. New generations will come and go, and new art impulses will beat, as the waves breaking from the Baltic, on the little pottery set on a rock and proud in its great achievements. The future, like the vessel in the furnace, is in the hands of Fate. Taking courage in both hands, the potter-sons of Denmark will in those yet unborn days carry on the great traditions. There is a great heritage for the sons of the days to come, and looking backward, they will place the laurel wreath on the brow of the masters who, in the old days and at the present era, have fought the good fight and won the guerdon of praise from potters in far-off lands who have paid homage to the art of the Three Blue Lines.

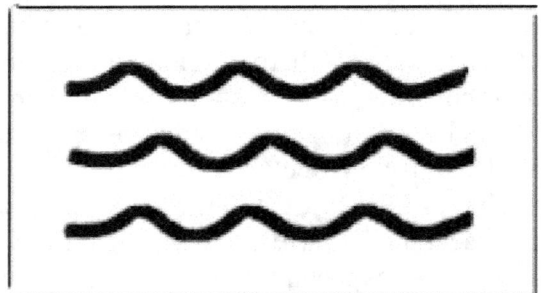

FINIS

Transcriber's Note

The background has been dropped out of some of the illustrations where it was easy. However many illustrations have the portions of the edge of the pottery in shadow and it is impossible to tell where boundary is, between the pottery and the background. In others, the background was left in the illustration for consistency.

Illustrations have been moved from their location in the original book so they do not break paragraphs. The links in the List of Illustrations point to the illustrations, not the cited page numbers.

Archaic and unusual spellings have been maintained as in the original book. Some spellings have been changed to bring conformance between the List of Illustrations, the body of the book and the Index. These are detailed in the table below and in the text.

In researching the correct spelling of Francesco Antonibon's name regarding his letter to Lady Charlotte Schreiber, it came to light that the cited work, "Marks and Monograms on Pottery and Porcelain" by William Chaffers does exist, but does not contain the cited information. A related work by the same author, "Marks and Monograms on European and Oriental Pottery and Porcelain with Historical Notices of Each Manufactory" contains the cited information. The citation has not been changed in the footnote in this book.

List of Illustrations Chapter II corrected Saucer. Eagle and Lamb Saucer. Water-god. Chapter II originally Saucers. Eagle and Lamb; Water-god. Chapter XI corrected Dish with tropical bird (*Christian Joachim*) Chapter XI originally Dish with tropical birds (*Christian Joachim*) **Index** Corrected Baÿer, J. C., the painter of the _Flora Danica_ service, Originally Bayer Corrected Foreign Workmen … Thomaschefsky, Originally Thomasefsky Corrected Frederiksborg Castle, vases at, Originally Fredericksborg Corrected Kändler of Meissen and his style, Originally Kandler Corrected Mehlhorn, a potter from Saxony, comes to Copenhagen, Originally Melhorn Corrected Ondrup (1779-1787), signature of, Originally Ondrop Corrected Schreiber, Lady Charlotte, letter from Francesco Antonibon to, Originally Antibon Corrected Shakesperean subjects (Copenhagen), Originally Shakesperian Corrected Thomaschefsky, Carl Fridrich, Originally Freidrich